Treasures In Dark Places

Debby Davis

All scripture Public Domaine

Cover picture
https://pixabay.com/fr/users/geralt-9301/?utm_source=link-attribution&utm_medium=referral&utm_campaign=image&utm_content=436138

Dedication

I dedicate this book to my Abba Father, the Lord God Almighty who has always been faithful to give me amazing treasures in all my dark places.

Preface

God spoke to Cyrus the King and said to him, "Behold I give you treasures in dark places. I began to ponder on this phrase and realized that there are treasures hidden in all the dark places of our lives. These treasures are not hidden away from us but are saved for moments when we desperately need to hear from God. When we find them their value becomes priceless as each is individually fashioned for each one who finds them.

I took liberties in dramatizing some of the Bible stories, but I believe I stayed true to the essence of the story and I have added the scriptures so you can be a Berean and see if what I said was scriptural true or not. I encourage you to read and reread the Bible stories as repetition is when they become alive and the scriptures reveal their own special treasures.

Some stories have had their names and personal details changed out of respect for their privacy.

Get out your shovels and pick axes, join me as we discover the Treasures in Dark Places.

Isaiah 45:3
I will give thee the treasures of darkness, and hidden riches of secret places, that thou mayest know that it is I, Jehovah, who call thee by thy name, even the God of Israel.ASV

I've had many opportunities to witness people suffering, from poverty-stricken children in developing nations to saints of God dying in hospital rooms. Each situation demands an answer to the question "why?" Why do innocent children suffer? Why do wonderful people who have spent their whole life serving God suffer? Why do you and I suffer? It's not a question easily answered.

Join me as we find the purpose for our suffering and discover the Treasures In Dark Places.

~~~~~~~~~

Covered with bandages hiding his bloody scabs and scars, the man limped his way to Jesus. He had almost given up all hope and wondered if he should end his life when he heard the healer was coming. The leper had to push his way through a crowd that didn't want him there. From all sides, they were slapping, kicking, and pushing him away, fearful that should he get too close, they would catch his disease. He wondered if he could get close enough to Jesus to speak to him, when suddenly he saw his chance, as the crowd parted just enough for him to hobble the last few feet. He fell before the healer and said, "Lord if you will, I know you can heal me."

Jesus responded, "I will." Immediately, the leper was healed. From that moment on, the man could feel pain.

This is one of many stories in the Bible about lepers. Leprosy is a bacterial disease that starts with numbness in the extremities, where eventually the victim loses all sense of feeling. Ultimately, they are disfigured from injuries that go unnoticed because the leper doesn't feel pain. Today, this disease is completely curable and yet the leading cause of death for those who have leprosy is suicide. Because lepers cannot feel pain, many are without hope and prefer death to a life without pain.

A very rare genetic disorder called Congenital Insensitivity to Pain or CIP also renders its sufferers without the ability to feel pain. Like those who suffer from leprosy, they also have a very high suicide rate. Steve Pete from Washington State USA is called The Man who Can't Feel Pain. He and his younger brother Chris were born with this disorder and the difficulties that they have suffered have been almost unbearable. Steve has broken over 70 bones in his body. Because his brother Chris could not feel pain, he unknowingly caused so much damage to his body that a doctor told him that by the time he was 30 he would most likely be in a wheelchair. The idea of living like that and never feeling pain was too much for him. He hung himself at 26 years old. Another disorder called Alexithymia is when a person can not feel emotional pain. This disorder also has a very high suicide rate with depression, confusion, feelings of emptiness, and panic attacks.

One common desire of those with these three afflictions have, is that of a long and healthy life. While most people run from pain, these people long for the ability to feel pain. They have no warning system that tells them they have broken a bone or burned their hands. They don't know when they have sprained their back or cut themselves. Most of these people would gladly trade their life of no pain for the ability to feel, because a life without feeling is no life at all.

I have heard many people comment to me they cannot cope with life because they can't handle the pain that they are in. They look at pain as something that should be avoided at all costs. Both physical and emotional pain have a purpose and a result that depends on our response. Is pain good or bad, or is pain really the issue in life that we think it is?

Perhaps pain isn't the enemy at all. Perhaps it is only a means to an end. Perhaps pain and suffering is a road map that leads us to Treasures in Dark Places.

Matthew 8:1-3
And when he was come down from the mountain, great multitudes followed him.
And behold, there came to him a leper and worshipped him, saying, Lord, if thou wilt, thou canst make me clean.
And he stretched forth his hand, and touched him, saying, I will; be thou made clean. And straightway his leprosy was cleansed. ASV

https://www.rd.com/article/pain-relievers/

https://www.healthline.com/health/autism/
alexithymia#symptoms

Table of Contents

Chapter 1

Joseph

How long he had been in the old dried-up, well, he didn't know. It was only a few hours, but already it felt like a lifetime. Joseph paced back and forth in the tiny space. He tried to sit, but he was too fidgety. All he wanted was to get out, but the pit was too deep. He tried yelling, but no one answered. Were they all really that mean? Didn't they care for him at all? He was their brother and yet he yelled until his voice gave out and no one responded. They didn't even come to check on him to see if he was all right.

He finally dropped to the ground. The sun had been beating on him until he could feel little blisters on his forehead. With no place to go, he put his head down on his knees, trying to protect his face from the sun. Suddenly, when he thought it couldn't get any worse, he heard a commotion at the top of the well. Shielding his eyes, he looked up, only to see strangers peering down at him. Who were they? It didn't take long before the mystery was solved. His brothers, sons of his father, had sold him. His own family had traded him for money. Not only that, but... before the traders took off with Joseph, one of his brothers yanked on the beautiful multicolored coat that his father had given him. He felt it tear as his brother ripped it from his grasp. "You won't need that where you're going." He said, and he walked away.

Joseph's whole life turned upside down. Deprived of enough water to drink and little food, he was broken, confused, and scared when he arrived in Egypt. Everything was different. He was a country boy. City life was like nothing he had ever known. No friends, no family. Even the food was a mystery to him. Besides that, he didn't know the language. The first few days were a nightmare. The favored son of wealthy herdsmen had become the least of all. Stripped of everything, he was now a slave. Little did the young man know that his life was following the course that would lead him straight to treasure.

He was sold to a government official named Potiphar and quickly adapted to life in Egypt. He didn't wallow in self-pity, but did his best to learn how to please his master. Soon Potiphar saw leadership abilities in Joseph and quickly promoted him. It wasn't long before Joseph was in charge of the entire house. He was doing his best in a difficult situation, unaware that he would soon lose everything again.

Potiphar had a beautiful wife who was used to getting her own way. Day after day, she looked at her husband's new slave. She admired his foreign looks, the accent of his voice, his well-toned arms. There was something special about him that attracted her. Ah yes, it was like the gods had smiled on him. She couldn't keep her eyes off of him until one day, when they were alone in the house, her passions could be ignored no longer. She grabbed Joseph, pulling him to her bedroom.

Joseph struggled against her. "Don't do this." he cried. "Your husband trusts me. I can't do this to him."

"Don't worry about him," she purred. "This can be our little secret. He doesn't need to know. Come. Come to my bedroom."

Her words felt like acid as they dripped from her mouth. She would not be stopped until Joseph pushed her away and fled from her grasp.

It wasn't until he reached his own room that he realized she had his coat. Trying to catch his breath, he dropped onto his bed and put his hands to his face. "Now what do I do?" he wondered. He knew things were about to get much worse for him.

Angry and humiliated, Potiphar's wife started screaming and waving Joseph's coat like a banner. "Look! Look! I have evidence against this Hebrew slave. While everyone was gone, he came to my room and made advances towards me. Look. I have proof. He even left his coat behind."

Whether or not Potiphar believed his wife, he had no choice but to have Joseph sent to prison. She was his wife, after all. And yet, even in prison, our young hero was in the perfect will of God.

Gone were the niceties Joseph had enjoyed in Potiphar's home. He no longer had a bed to sleep on, and the food was terrible. That is, if you could call the slop, they were fed food. The prison was little more than a hole in the ground with little light. Rats and snakes lived there too and competed for their food. However, this was more of a political prison than one for hardened criminals and so the food and liberties were a little better than in other prisons.

Regardless of Jospeh's location, the favor of God still rested upon him, and soon he was in charge of the whole prison. Twelve, perhaps thirteen years passed, and the future looked to promise the same. Was there any way out? Other prisoners came and went, and yet no one ever came looking for Joseph. His father surely thought he was dead. No one else cared. He was all alone. And yet God was with the young man. There was no doubt. He became well known for his honesty and hard work. He even interpreted dreams for other prisoners. "Remember me," he would say to them as they were released. "When you get out of here, remember me." But no one did.

Suddenly, one day, Joseph heard people calling his name. Who would look for me with such urgency, he wondered? Grabbed by muscular arms and practically carried out of the prison, they led him to the bathhouse, where others scrubbed on his skin and trimmed his hair. Someone dumped some fragrant oils on his skin and rubbed them in. New clothes and sandals were put on his feet. What was going on he could not tell, nor in his wildest dreams could he imagine what the rest of the day held.

Several years passed. Joseph had interpreted Pharaoh's dreams and because of the wisdom God had given him, he became the most powerful men in the land, second only to

16

Pharaoh. Everything about Joseph changed: his appearance, his voice, his mannerisms, even his name. He had not only the favor of God in his life but also the favor of man. Everyone respected him. He had no needs, as every wish of his was carried out. People bowed before him when they entered a room and bowed as they left. Joseph had, at his disposal, all the riches of Egypt. He had a family, servants, employees, and guards. What he didn't have were his brothers and his dad.

Then suddenly, standing before him, were faces he had not seen since he was a teenager. There was Reuben, Simeon, Levi, Judah, Issachar, Zebulun, Gad, Asher, Dan, and Naphtali all bowing before him, not knowing who he was. Oh, but he knew them, that was for sure - he recognized them all. Then, with the forgiveness developed within him while he suffered, he brought them to Egypt, and cared for them. He didn't respond to them in the way they deserved, no he responded by sharing his treasure.

So you may ask, what treasures did Joseph find in his dark places? His treasure had many layers. He learned to hear God's voice and found favor and peace with God and man. He saved Egypt and many other nations from famine. Without Joseph's dark places, the entire nation of Israel would have died. Without the treasure Joseph found, Jesus the Messiah would not have been born. No one would know salvation. There would be no redemption. There would be no relationship with God for us today as we know it.

Yes, there was a reason Joseph suffered. I imagine that a day never went by when he didn't cry out to the Lord for his father. Surely he had lonely and fearful nights, as he was only a child when he had been sold into slavery. He had no comforts; no friends; no family; living alone in a faraway place with only his God. He trusted God, much like David, who wrote in Psalm 31, that his life was in the hands of the Lord.

Psalm 31:12-15

I am forgotten as a dead man out of mind: I am like a broken vessel.
For I have heard the defaming of many, Terror on every side: While they took counsel together against me, they devised to take away my life.
But I trusted in thee, O Jehovah: I said, Thou art my God.
My times are in thy hand: Deliver me from the hand of mine enemies, and from them that persecute me.ASV

While you may never be forced to live in a prison, or faced with the troubles that Joseph faced, the treasure still awaits those who seek after it. Joseph was ridiculed, bullied, lied about, rejected, sold, and forgotten by those he loved and trusted. Perhaps, like him, you have been rejected by your family, or by choice you have moved far away and you struggle with loneliness. Perhaps people have lied about you and you are in your own prison. Not all prisons are the same, some are made of shame and others regret. If you are lonely or feel ashamed, look for the treasure that God has hidden in your dark place. There is a day coming when you will come out of your troubles, when you will understand why you have suffered. But in the meantime, look for treasure. Don't leave your dark place without it. Joseph came out and saved a nation. He came out without revenge or casting blame. And when his father died and his brothers were afraid of what Joseph might do to them for selling him, Joseph's response was, "What you intended for evil, God turned for good. Don't be afraid. I will take care of you and your families. You have nothing to fear." Take those words to heart, my friend. What Satan has done to you was meant for evil, but God has turned those things into your treasures of dark places.

Genesis 50:19-21

And Joseph said unto them, Fear not: for am I in the place of God?
And as for you, ye meant evil against me; but God meant it for good, to bring to pass, as it is this day, to save much people alive.
Now therefore fear ye not: I will nourish you, and your little ones. And he comforted them, and spake kindly unto them.ASV

Chapter 2
The Prophesy

The night was dark, and the stars were twinkling in the sky as he wandered back to his flock of sheep. The sound of baaing lambs settled on him like a warm blanket. He was home among his wooly friends. He leaned up against a gnarly tree and pulled out his harp and started to sing. His mind was so full of the day's events that he couldn't think straight. What he needed most was to settle his spirit. "Bless the Lord, oh my soul. Bless his name. Holy holy is his name, oh my soul. Bless his holy name." He often sang when he was confused, and tonight, more than any other night in his life, he was confused. Sliding down the side of the tree, he sat, pulling one of his lambs close to him. Pushing his nose into the fluffy wool, he took a deep breath. He knew all the sheep, but this little one was his favorite. Just holding him brought comfort.

Playing the day's events over again in his mind, he sorted it all out. "Lord God, is this true? Of course it is true. The prophet would not have come if it wasn't true. The old man always speaks for you, Lord. And he is never wrong. But the king? Me?"

Then his thoughts raced again. What does it feel like to be a king? I don't feel any different. Should I tell my friends? What will they say? And King Saul? What will he say? How does one go about becoming a king? Do I get a crown? A sword? The thoughts didn't stop - they seemed to run in circles in his mind. When the sun rose in the sky and there was no more danger to his sheep from the creatures of the night, David finally closed his eyes and slept.

One would think that after such a powerful word from God, that life would be all smooth sailing for the lad who would be king. But no. The minute the prophet spoke the Word of God, David's life turned upside down. He hadn't gone looking for the prophetic word. He wasn't expecting it, but the Prophet Samuel assured him that God had made him king. King? "Why me?" He wondered. After all, he was just a boy. The questions flooded his mind and, try as he might, he couldn't make them go away. How could he become the king? When would it happen? Why would God choose him? And yet he did.

Soon after, David found himself in the employ of the reigning monarch, King Saul. He fought a giant and killed him. Then killed many more enemy soldiers - many, many more than even the king had killed. All the girls in the streets swooned when they saw him, and they sang songs about his victories. If he thought this would impress Saul, he was wrong. The king suffered from madness brought on by his broken relationship with the Almighty. He wanted the victories David brought him, but jealous fits of rage came over him until he vowed to kill the young man that he swore he loved like a son.

David must have wondered how it could it be, that after such a wonderful prophetic word, that he was to endure so much trouble? Wandering about the countryside, David hid. He loved King Saul, risking his life for the sake of his king. He would do anything for that man. Yet what he received in return was jealous hatred, rejection, and loss. Could it be that this is the way prophetic words come to pass?

Often, prophetic words come with a shovel. They're a treasure that doesn't come to pass without digging for it, and digging is hard work. Many people, after receiving a word of encouragement, a prophetic word, or words they have read in their Bible, think that these words come to pass all by themselves. While it is possible for God to change a person's life overnight, because of a prophetic word, it is seldom the way it happens. Sincere people believing that God is going to do something in their life often become frustrated when it doesn't happen in the timing or the way they believed it would. They get blown away and some are tragically devastated. Instead of believing in the prophetic promise, they suffer and decide that the word was wrong. They walk away from their promise from God, because they misunderstand the purpose of their suffering between the prophecy and its fulfillment.

Throughout my life, I had read many books about God's faithfulness to those called to the mission field. My church often invited missionaries to visit, tell their stories, and show pictures they projected on a screen, using a funny little machine they called a slide projector. Fred and I received many prophetic words that assured us we should go into missionary work. We were excited at the prospect and my mind whirled with the imagination of living the "missionary dream." The last thing I expected was to fall headfirst into a crisis.

We were returning from a pastor's conference late at night and heard our telephone answering machine beeping with dozens of calls and messages. They were all from the same person, my doctor. "Call me as soon as you get this message. I need to speak to you right now. It is urgent." Shaking, I picked up the phone.

Cancer. The very word spoke terror to my entire being. Inside I was screaming, "Why me? How could this be happening? Now what? How does this fit with our prophetic words? I don't understand - this can't be happening. Things like this aren't supposed to happen to me. I don't understand. I don't understand. The word cancer paralyzed me like a crushing weight. In the middle of those first few days when I found out I had cancer, God spoke to me. It took me a while to hear him. I was so caught up with those bad words that the good words, the Good News from Heaven, were drowned out, but soon my spirit calmed and I heard God speak.

"Will you go too?"

I knew right away that those were the same words Jesus spoke to Peter when many of his disciples were offended at his teachings and walked away from him. Jesus looked at Peter and said, "Will you go too?" Like Peter, I answered, "No Lord, for you alone have the words of eternal life. I have no other place to go. I will not leave."

In that moment, Jesus gave me a treasure. He said, "Now you have faith."

"Now I have faith? What does that mean?" I wondered.

He responded to my heart, "Faith is not faith until it has been tried, and faith has not been tried until it has been offended and still believes." I had been offended that I had gotten sick. My faith was offended when I didn't understand why I had cancer. My faith in Divine healing was offended when I wasn't miraculously healed and needed surgery. I was offended, but I didn't leave. How could I leave the one I loved? How could I stop walking with God just because I didn't understand? I had no other place to go. No, I wouldn't leave. I took my shovel and scooped up my treasure. I had faith.

John 6:66-69
Upon this many of his disciples went back,
and walked no more with him.
Jesus said therefore unto the twelve,
Would ye also go away?
Simon Peter answered him, Lord, to whom shall we go?
thou hast the words of eternal life.
And we have believed and know that thou art the Holy One
of God. ASV

I never came to a full understanding of why I got cancer and had to go through difficult medical treatments, but I received treasure worth so much more than anything I lost to cancer. I received an understanding of faith that I never knew before. Husbands and wives, when they recite their vows on their wedding day, declare their faith. They make declarations of faith, promising they will not leave the other, whether they face sickness or poverty. They promise their faith, but they don't prove their faith until after many years of life together. Offending and forgiving each other, they remain together with their powerfully maturing faith. Faith to another, whether to God, friends, church fellowship, business, or marriage, isn't faith until it is tried - offended and stays in that relationship. Eventually, Fred and I became missionaries, and I have preached this treasured faith concept all over the world, and it has touched many lives.

Acts 16:16-24

And it came to pass, as we were going to the place of prayer, that a certain maid having a spirit of divination met us, who brought her masters much gain by soothsaying. The same following after Paul and us cried out, saying, These men are servants of the Most High God, who proclaim unto you the way of salvation. And this she did for many days. But Paul, being sore troubled, turned and said to the spirit, I charge thee in the name of Jesus Christ to come out of her. And it came out that very hour. But when her masters saw that the hope of their gain was gone, they laid hold on Paul and Silas, and dragged them into the marketplace before the rulers, and when they had brought them unto the magistrates, they said, These men, being Jews, do exceedingly trouble our city, and set forth customs which it is not lawful for us to receive, or to observe, being Romans.

And the multitude rose up together against them: and the magistrates rent their garments off them, and commanded to beat them with rods.
And when they had laid many stripes upon them, they cast them into prison, charging the jailor to keep them safely: who, having received such a charge, cast them into the inner prison, and made their feet fast in the stocks. ASV

Look at the lives of Paul and Silas. They went to Mesopotamia, because they had a "word from God." In a prophetic dream, a man from Mesopotamia came to Paul and said, "come to Mesopotamia and help us." They packed their bags and went to Mesopotamia. While they were there, they preached the Gospel, doing what God called them to do. Unfortunately, a woman possessed of a devil followed them as they preached, causing a commotion. Paul, weary of her outbursts, cast the demon out of her. When the men who profited from her fortune-telling discovered she could no longer call upon her demons, they angrily accused Paul and Silas of causing riots and they were beaten and thrown into prison.

Acts 16:25-26
But about midnight Paul and Silas were praying and singing hymns unto God, and the prisoners were listening to them;
and suddenly there was a great earthquake, so that the foundations of the prison-house were shaken: and immediately all the doors were opened, and every one's bands were loosed. ASV

Too often, when bad things happen to us, we errantly assume that we have done something wrong. In the story of Paul and Silas, nothing could be further from the truth. They seemed unfazed by their surroundings and the beatings they received. At midnight, when the prison was the darkest, and the air was heavy, they sang. They praised the Lord with their whole hearts, ignoring the pain of their beaten bodies. They didn't allow their situation to dictate their response. Then something wonderful happened. As they were worshiping the Lord, the earth trembled violently where even the foundations of the prison were moved. The chains broke off from all the prisoners, and the doors flew open. Imagine what it must have been like, when one minute you are chained - unable to escape, and the next minute you are free.

Paul and Silas had done nothing wrong, and at the midnight hour, when most people would have given up and succumbed to depression and defeat, Paul and Silas were set free. Not only that, but they led their jailer and his complete family to Jesus. I believe this jailer was the man in Paul's dreams. In God's timing, in his plan, the prophetic dream came to pass. But it never would have happened had Paul and Silas not been beaten and thrown into jail.

Not everything that looks bad is bad. Not everything that hurts you happen because you did something wrong. Sometimes God has a bigger plan that he has not shared with you. David suffered because of the prophetic word, and Paul and Silas suffered because of their prophetic dream. All three men were righteous and blameless, and yet they suffered. So why do bad things happen to good people? Things like cancer, heart attacks, broken marriages, the death of a loved one happen to the just and the unjust. When they happen, we say, "this shouldn't have happened to me. I love God with all of my heart. I have done exactly what God wanted me to do and this shouldn't have happened." While there is truth to that statement, it is not the whole truth. Bad things happen to good people to propel them into their destiny.

If David hadn't been anointed by the Prophet Samuel to be the next king over God's people, he never would have become king, and yet he suffered between the spoken prophecy and its fulfillment. Every day, he had to remind himself of what God said through the prophet. Every day, by faith, he had to put one foot in front of the other. Does this mean he didn't wonder about that word? No. He often spoke in the Psalms of hiding in the Lord. He knew where to take refuge when it seemed like the entire world was against him. He saw it as a time of testing, one that he eventually passed. The Kingdom of God was David's treasure. When he was a young man, he probably thought his kingdom was only for the family of Israel, but no, the treasure he gained was for the eternal Kingdom of God. He cried out to the Lord in his struggles and worshiped the Lord in his pain. Even when it seemed everyone had failed him, he never gave up his quest for treasure. Somehow, in God's incredible way, he turned David's kingdom from a time constrained kingdom to one that would last forever.

2 Samuel 7:16-17
And thy house and thy kingdom shall be made sure for ever before thee: thy throne shall be established for ever.

According to all these words, and according to all this
vision, so did Nathan speak unto David. ASV

Psalm 5:11-12
But let all those that take refuge in thee rejoice, Let them
ever shout for joy, because thou defendest them: Let them
also that love thy name be joyful in thee.
For thou wilt bless the righteous; O Jehovah, thou wilt
compass him with favor as with a shield. ASV

Psalm 11:5
"Jehovah trieth the righteous; But the wicked and him that
loveth violence his soul hateth.ASV

Paul and Silas were also being tested. Would they grumble
and complain? Would they succumb to their beatings and
whimper all night? No, they rejoiced. They knew that
their pain and suffering were not a sign that God had
rejected them. No, the situation was necessary for them
and expected. Paul said in Colossians that it was through
the times when he suffered he found a mystery. He found a
treasure in his dark place, hidden inside of the dark,
oppressive prison, a treasure that needed to be dug out.
Praise and worship became Paul's shovel. He and Silas
dug and dug for treasure with their worship until the earth
could hide it no longer.

Colossians 1:24-26
Now I rejoice in my sufferings for your sake, and fill up on
my part that which is lacking of the afflictions of Christ in
my flesh for his body's sake, which is the church;

whereof I was made a minister, according to the
dispensation of God which was given me to you-ward, to
fulfil the word of God,
even the mystery which hath been hid for ages and
generations: but now hath it been manifested to his saints,
ASV

Chapter 3
The Cave

Having experienced the epic climax of his career, the prophet wallowed in despair. Frustration dogged him like a rabid hound looking for someone to pick a fight with. One would think Elijah would be happy, feeling at the top of his game, but no. He was depressed and anxious, and he fought demons of suicide. After defeating four hundred and fifty prophets of Baal, he should have felt energized and invincible. But one word from the king's wife Jezebel, threatening to kill him for what he had done, and all his hope and joy was lost. Elijah felt rejection, and it had a profound effect on him. He wanted to die.

The angel of the Lord came to him and said, "Wake up, get ready, and prepare for a journey." God was sending Elijah to Mount Horeb, the mountain of God, the place where Moses received the Ten Commandments. So Elijah made the journey that took him forty days and forty nights. A musty, old cave became his home while he waited for God to speak. Suddenly he heard, "What are you doing, Elijah? What's going on with you? Why are you so upset?"

Elijah was incredulous at the question. "What do you mean, why am I so upset? I dedicated myself to you, serving you, and speaking to your people, the very ones who have forsaken your covenant. They killed all of your prophets and now they are trying to kill me. I'm the only one left. I am alone, utterly and completely alone. Isn't it obvious why I'm upset?"

God's response? "Stand on the mountain and wait for me." There is much unsaid and much implied in that statement. God was already speaking to Elijah and yet, instead of continuing the conversation, he tells this frustrated prophet to stand on the mountain and wait. Waiting on God is not an unusual request. So he stood at the edge of the cave. Even though he was wrapped in his outer cloak, he shivered while depression fell upon him like a wet blanket. His mind told him he shouldn't be so frustrated. Hadn't God done amazing things in his life? What about the miracles he had seen? He had walked with God and talked to him. Their conversations had been intimate. No one had a relationship with God like he had, and yet he felt alone. Sad and melancholy, he stood, crying to his God, "I'm alone. No one understands me. I have served you my whole life. Oh, why do I feel this way?"

Suddenly there was a wind and an earthquake. Elijah was sure God was speaking in the earthquake, but there was no word from God when the earth stopped trembling. Then there was a fire. Perhaps God was in the fire, but no. There was no word from God. He was looking in all the wrong places.

Then in the quiet; in a whisper, God spoke to him. "What are you doing here?" God asked.

In his mind he thought, "What am I doing here? What? You told me to come, that is why I am here," but those words didn't come out of his mouth. How does one talk back to God?

"I have spent my whole life serving you. With great passion, I have done everything you have asked of me, and yet, the people don't care. They don't serve you. Even the great miracles you have done have not changed them; I'm all alone. No one stands with me. All the prophets are dead. I'm all alone. People are trying to kill me, and I feel like giving up. What's the use of going on?"

Gently, God whispered to Elijah. "You are not alone. There are seven thousand who stand with you. I am with you, and I still have a job for you to do. Don't give up."

Elijah found treasure in the cave of despair, a most solitary place, alone, far from any comfort. God's response was treasure. "Go to the wilderness of Damascus. I have found a man to take your place." And his troubles? Oh, he left them in the cave of despair,

Elisha became his constant companion, following him wherever he went. As long as Elijah was living on the earth, he was never alone again. Several years went by, and thoughts of dying were now gone. As a matter of fact, Elijah never did die. In a whirlwind, God took him up to Heaven in a flaming chariot pulled along by horses of fire.

1 Kings 19:9-18

And he came thither unto a cave, and lodged there; and, behold, the word of Jehovah came to him, and he said unto him, What doest thou here, Elijah?

And he said, I have been very jealous for Jehovah, the God of hosts; for the children of Israel have forsaken thy covenant, thrown down thine altars, and slain thy prophets with the sword: and I, even I only, am left; and they seek my life, to take it away.

And he said, Go forth, and stand upon the mount before Jehovah. And, behold, Jehovah passed by, and a great and strong wind rent the mountains, and brake in pieces the rocks before Jehovah; but Jehovah was not in the wind: and after the wind an earthquake; but Jehovah was not in the earthquake:

and after the earthquake a fire; but Jehovah was not in the fire: and after the fire a still small voice.

And it was so, when Elijah heard it, that he wrapped his face in his mantle, and went out, and stood in the entrance of the cave. And, behold, there came a voice unto him, and said, What doest thou here, Elijah?

And he said, I have been very jealous for Jehovah, the God of hosts; for the children of Israel have forsaken thy covenant, thrown down thine altars, and slain thy prophets with the sword; and I, even I only, am left; and they seek my life, to take it away.

And Jehovah said unto him, Go, return on thy way to the wilderness of Damascus: and when thou comest, thou shalt anoint Hazael to be king over Syria;

and Jehu the son of Nimshi shalt thou anoint to be king over Israel; and Elisha the son of Shaphat of Abel-meholah shalt thou anoint to be prophet in thy room.

*And it shall come to pass, that him that escapeth from the
sword of Hazael shall Jehu slay; and him that escapeth
from the sword of Jehu shall Elisha slay.
Yet will I leave me seven thousand in Israel, all the knees
which have not bowed unto Baal, and every mouth which
hath not kissed him. ASV*

Romans 11:1-4

*I say then, Did God cast off his people? God forbid. For I
also am an Israelite, of the seed of Abraham, of the tribe of
Benjamin.
God did not cast off his people which he foreknew. Or know
ye not what the scripture saith of Elijah? how he pleadeth
with God against Israel:
Lord, they have killed thy prophets, they have digged down
thine altars; and I am left alone, and they seek my life.
But what saith the answer of God unto him? I have left for
myself seven thousand men, who have not bowed the knee
to Baal. ASV*

Elijah, one of the greatest prophets to have ever lived,
suffered from the depression of rejection. He forgot who he
was. He forgot the power of his God, and he felt all alone.
It is often when we are struggling and suffering all alone
that God sees fit to tell us to wait for him. Elijah felt like
that, even though we know God told him there were seven
thousand others like him. Those feelings brought about a
dreadful, depressive despair that worked away at him until
he didn't want to live any longer. Have you ever felt like
that? Do you feel lonely even though you know there are
people in your life? Have you felt like giving up, forgetting
the miracles and blessings that God has done for you? If
the great prophet Elijah suffered from depression, it is not

unusual that the devil would try to afflict us in the same way.

Scientists have discovered that physical pain and rejection are processed in the brain the same way. While testing the reaction of the brain to rejection, they gave people Tylenol before asking them to recall situations where they were rejected. Those who received the Tylenol had a significant reduction of their emotional pain.* It is no wonder rejection is one of the hardest feelings to deal with.

Many Christians suffer from rejection-depression and don't know it. They plod on day after day, and suddenly the joy of the Lord is gone. Apathetic and weary, they put one foot in front of the other out of habit, but have lost their passion and feel alone. Spiritual depression falls upon them like it did Elijah. They call out to God, hoping for a sign from heaven. "If only God would speak to me," they cry. So they look for God's voice in the thunders and shakings of their emotions. They look at the fires of life. They search in all the wrong places to hear God's voice. Is God there? Yes, but he speaks in the whispers. God's response is in a quiet place. God is whispering, "come close to me because I am the good shepherd. I will lead you to the still waters and bring you to a place of rest. Come close to me. You are not alone."

Today, we see political powers shaken to their roots. Wars, natural disasters and riots are happening around the world, while fires burn, and the sick are dying. Many cry out, "Where is God? Where is he? I feel all alone, and I need a word from God. I need it now! Doesn't God care?"

Compare Elijah's cave experience with David. Running for his life, David hid among the caves, sometimes with others who were also running from King Saul, and sometimes alone. These things never would have happened if he weren't a threat to King Saul. He wouldn't be a threat if he hadn't been anointed to be king. That one prophetic action had set his world on fire, and he had no choice but to go on. Never retreating, never giving up, David ran and hid, coming out to fight Israel's enemies while running from the King he called Father.

David was in the middle of the plan of God and yet everything seemed against him. No matter how hard he tried, no matter how hard he fought for the king, no matter how much he worshiped God, he often felt alone and feared the traps in his path.

Psalm 142
I cry with my voice unto Jehovah; With my voice unto Jehovah do I make supplication.
I pour out my complaint before him; I show before him my trouble.
When my spirit was overwhelmed within me, Thou knewest my path. In the way wherein I walk Have they hidden a snare for me.
Look on my right hand, and see; For there is no man that knoweth me: Refuge hath failed me; No man careth for my soul.
I cried unto thee, O Jehovah; I said, Thou art my refuge, My portion in the land of the living.
Attend unto my cry; For I am brought very low: Deliver me from my persecutors; For they are stronger than I.

Bring my soul out of prison, That I may give thanks unto thy name: The righteous shall compass me about; For thou wilt deal bountifully with me. ASV

As we look at Psalm 142, we see David crying out to the Lord, feeling hopeless and begging God to help him. He is hiding in a cave, lonely and suffering. "Does anyone care?" he asks. Hunted like an animal and hanging on his one sure thread of hope, he believed God would rescue him.

Can you imagine living like that? The caves David lived in were limestone caves that were deep and dark, with some areas so shallow, that sometimes, it was hard even to crawl into, while other areas were cavernous with dangerous drop offs that would catch someone unknowingly to tumble to their death. The air was often stale and humid, with snakes, bats, and scorpions crawling about. Even so, caves were like a second home to shepherds. They often cared for their sheep by a nearby cave, gathering the flock inside to protect them from the cold while the shepherd slept near the entrance lest a hungry fox or lion should wander in and kill his flock. For David, this was home. He was weary and filled with despair from running, yet he found treasures in his caves. They became his secret place, and he wrote several Psalms in those dark and musty places.

Let's look at Psalm 57.

Psalm 57
Be merciful unto me, O God, be merciful unto me; For my soul taketh refuge in thee: Yea, in the shadow of thy wings will I take refuge, Until these calamities be overpast.

40

*I will cry unto God Most High, Unto God that performeth
all things for me.
He will send from heaven, and save me, When he that
would swallow me up reproacheth; Selah God will send
forth his lovingkindness and his truth.
My soul is among lions; I lie among them that are set on
fire, Even the sons of men, whose teeth are spears and
arrows, And their tongue a sharp sword.
Be thou exalted, O God, above the heavens; Let thy glory
be above all the earth.
They have prepared a net for my steps; My soul is bowed
down: They have digged a pit before me; They are fallen
into the midst thereof themselves. Selah
My heart is fixed, O God, my heart is fixed: I will sing, yea,
I will sing praises.
Awake up, my glory; Awake, psaltery and harp: I myself
will awake right early.
I will give thanks unto thee, O Lord, among the peoples: I
will sing praises unto thee among the nations.
For thy lovingkindness is great unto the heavens, And thy
truth unto the skies.
Be thou exalted, O God, above the heavens; Let thy glory
be above all the earth. ASV*

David said he was hiding under God's wings. Remember,
he was in a damp, dark, solitary cave, but he knew that
there was more to the cave than what he could see with his
eyes. He was hidden in God. Caves were his secret place.
They were the place he could go to hide in God and look
for treasure. He experienced worship and praise in these
dark places. Love that was deeper and higher than he could
express flooded his heart. The secret place was where he
was rejuvenated and strengthened. He would hunker down

and regroup, searching his heart and making sure he was right before God. Then, in the safety of his cave, he would prepare his next step. David didn't focus on his suffering. He focused on what God could do for him. Oh yes, sometimes he struggled, but as he worshiped God, his focus changed from his problems to worshiping God. He found the riches of worship in his suffering and discovered that it was the key to coming out of fear and depression. He used it often in his life. It was a treasure that he found in his dark places. It was his habit. When Absalom stole the kingdom from his father David, he sought advice from Hushai the Arkite about how he should pursue his father. Hushai responded with, "You know your dad. He's probably in a cave by now."

2 Samuel 17:8-9
Hushai said moreover, Thou knowest thy father and his men, that they are mighty men, and they are chafed in their minds, as a bear robbed of her whelps in the field; and thy father is a man of war, and will not lodge with the people. Behold, he is hid now in some pit (cave), or in some other place: and it will come to pass, when some of them are fallen at the first, that whosoever heareth it will say, There is a slaughter among the people that follow Absalom. ASV

A few years ago, I was going through a difficult time and I desperately needed a hiding place, a place where I could be alone with God. I chose one closet in my house that was set under a staircase. I pulled out all the coats and jackets that were stored there, and replaced them with a couple of pillows, a small lamp, and my Bible. That became my place to pray and be alone with God. Just the act of going in and closing the door brought peace to my heart. That closet was my cave, and while I was there, I went looking for treasure. I looked for God's reassurance and his love. I looked for strength to face my difficulties and peace that would overcome my distress.

Have you suffered rejection? Are you dealing with the profound feelings of being rejected, like Elijah and David? Have you been rejected by a parent or a child? Did your best friend walk away from you? Find a secret place where you can give the Lord your sadness and despair. Almost anyplace can be your cave if it is where you can be alone with God. Some people run with headphones on to shut off the sounds of the world, others have a park, a favorite tree to sit under, a closet, attic, or basement. Ask God to help you. He will. And once you have found your hiding place, start digging for treasure. Stop feeling sorry for yourself and focus on what God has done for you and remind yourself of his promises. There is a treasure hidden there if you will look. All you have to do is dig. And when you find it… go out, live your life and leave your troubles in the cave of despair.

*https://www.psychologytoday.com/us/blog/the-squeaky-wheel/201307/10-surprising-facts-about-rejection

Chapter 4
What Is Hard

It was decided. The father looked at his son and asked, "Are you ready? Are you sure you want to go through with this?"

The son lifted his head with tears in his eyes. "Yes, I am sure. There is nothing I wouldn't do for them."

In the flash of a moment that also seemed like an eternity, the son was born in a little town called Bethlehem. Jesus chose to do what was hard.

Hard things can be very fearful. Many are anxious about their future solely because they fear the unknown hard thing. Even though Jesus knew he had been born to die, even though he knew the desired outcome, he too feared the hard thing as he wept in the garden, "Oh Father, if it is in any way possible, for me to not have to go to the cross in this way, please get me out of this situation. Nevertheless, I will do your will and not mine."

Mark 14:36

And he said, Abba, Father, all things are possible unto thee; remove this cup from me: howbeit not what I will, but what thou wilt. ASV

Saul was not a stranger to hard things. He had given his life to study God's word. From a small boy, he had dedicated himself to the Almighty. He had a pretty good life. Honored among all the great religious leaders in the temple, he was well respected and known for being passionate about serving God. Oh yes, he was very passionate. All he wanted to do was to hunt down everybody who was a follower of Jesus. It was his mission, and he would chain every last one of them, put them in prison, and see them die. But while he was on his mission, suddenly a light from heaven shined upon him and in the light was a voice that said, "Saul. Saul. What are you doing? Why are you persecuting me?"

In that moment, Saul, who would one day become the great Apostle Paul, was struck blind. He cried out, "Who are you? Who… who are you?"

The answer? "I am Jesus, the one that you have been persecuting. I am the one that you have waged war against!" Even the men traveling with Paul were struck speechless. The voice had come from heaven and Saul, the tyrant of the early church, could not deny that he had heard the voice of God. Then he was instructed to go on to the city where he would be told what to do.

Saul (Paul) spent the next three days praying. Shaking, he desperately needed a word from God. What had happened to him? Why was he blind? It was a darkness he had never experienced before. Would he never see again? And how did Jesus speak to him? He didn't understand. He had great zeal for The Almighty, but never in his wildest dreams did he imagine he was wrong about Jesus. So he prayed until in a vision he saw a man named Ananias. Ananias would come and pray for him and he would see again. It wasn't long after Ananias prayed for Saul that he could be seen in the synagogue and on the streets, proclaiming that Jesus was the Son of God. Now the hunter became the hunted.

He didn't start out as the great apostle, Paul. No, he went through hard times before he became the apostle. He endured multiple shipwrecks and spent a day and night in the open sea. Our apostle in the making was snake bit, in danger of robbers, flogged, beaten, and stoned. Persecuted by the Romans, Jews, and Christians, he was hunted down like an animal and often had to flee an area in secrecy. Paul knew what it was like to pay the price of apostleship. It came as a treasure birthed in hard things.

2Corinthians 11:21-28

I speak by way of disparagement, as though we had been weak. Yet whereinsoever any is bold (I speak in foolishness), I am bold also.
Are they Hebrews? so am I. Are they Israelites? so am I. Are they the seed of Abraham? so am I.
Are they ministers of Christ? (I speak as one beside himself) I more; in labors more abundantly, in prisons more abundantly, in stripes above measure, in deaths oft.
Of the Jews five times received I forty stripes save one.

Thrice was I beaten with rods, once was I stoned, thrice I
suffered shipwreck, a night and
a day have I been in the deep;
in journeyings often, in perils of rivers, in perils of robbers,
in perils from my countrymen, in perils from the Gentiles,
in perils in the city, in perils in the wilderness, in perils in
the sea, in perils among false brethren;
in labor and travail, in watchings often, in hunger and
thirst, in fastings often, in cold and nakedness.
Besides those things that are without, there is that which
presseth upon me daily, anxiety for all the churches. ASV

Almost no one looks forward to the hard situations of life, and yet most welcome the rewards. It's human nature to look for the easy way to achieve recognition, money, or position, but for those who do it the hard way, for those who will pay the price, there is a glorious reward. People who have lofty aspirations do hard things to achieve their goals. A concert pianist practices days, sometimes years, for one concert opportunity and the hope of a position in an orchestra. A young girl who dreams of being a world class gymnast goes to the gym before the sun is up just to practice before school. Often skipping social events to practice more, she seldom indulges in burgers or pizzas, and late nights with friends. She does the hard thing. Would be doctors, an engineer, or a successful businessman will set aside years to go to school, get the degree, hone their abilities, and achieve their goals. They do hard things. If it wasn't hard, everyone would do it.

There are people who pretend to be doctors or lawyers or someone with some kind of "hard earned degree" who are caught and sent to jail because it's illegal to pretend to have these positions without paying the hard price. Those who pretend without doing the work, without being judged, tried and found to be worthy of that position, are cheaters and their life is a life of Illusion. It's not a real life. Frank Abagnale Jr. was one such imposter in the 1970s. He pretended to be a pilot, doctor, lawyer, and an assistant state attorney general. It seemed there was no one he couldn't pretend to be. However, he had not earned the right to these professions. He was living the life of a fraud. The FBI went on a manhunt looking for him, and eventually he was arrested because he had not earned the right to be called a pilot, a doctor, a lawyer, or whatever else he pretended to be.

God has called us to pay the price. He is not looking for frauds. He is looking for genuine treasure hunters who will do hard things in order to live a fulfilled life. So what are these hard things you may ask? They are many, such as going to school and getting a degree, becoming an apprentice-following in someone's footsteps, serving one another in love, sacrificing time, money, and even relationships for the sake of one's desired goal. It is walking in faith-sometimes alone, and being rejected by friends and family for the sake of your relationship with Christ. It is treasure hunting.

Yes, the hard thing is fearful. No one said the hard thing would not be hard. Sometimes it is painful to the point of despair and many give up before they receive their hard sought after treasure. When you do the right thing, the treasure opens doors for you. When you do what is hard, it gives you a great reward. It changes your situation. Hard things bring treasure troves of revelation, knowledge, education, and position. They provide finances, respect, and sometimes even a title. But none of these mean anything, if you didn't earn it, if you didn't do the hard thing.

In the book of Acts, there is a story of the seven sons of a man named Sceva. They were trying to cast demons out of someone. This story is interesting because when they talked to the evil spirits, they said, "We command you to leave this man in the name of Jesus who Paul talks about."

The response of the evil spirits was this: "We know Jesus and we know Paul, but you are a fraud. We don't know you!"

The spirits refused to leave the possessed person, and jumped all over Sceva's sons, attacking the imposters, tearing their clothes off. Their naked bodies, while exposed for everyone to see, also exposed their lack of relationship with Jesus - they were frauds. The hard thing was not done. They had not died to self and given their lives to Jesus. They wanted to cast out demons, but they were not willing to pay the price to get the treasure needed to have authority over these evil spirits.

Acts 19:13-16
But certain also of the strolling Jews, exorcists, took upon them to name over them that had the evil spirits the name of the Lord Jesus, saying, I adjure you by Jesus whom Paul preacheth.
And there were seven sons of one Sceva, a Jew, a chief priest, who did this.

And the evil spirit answered and said unto them, Jesus I know, and Paul I know, but who are ye?
And the man in whom the evil spirit was leaped on them, and mastered both of them, and prevailed against them, so that they fled out of that house naked and wounded. ASV

2 Samuel 24:24
And the king said unto Araunah, Nay; but I will verily buy it of thee at a price. Neither will I offer burnt-offerings unto Jehovah my God which cost me nothing. So David bought the threshing-floor and the oxen for fifty shekels of silver. ASV

That was how King David felt. He wanted to build an alter and make a sacrifice to the Lord. Araunah had the perfect threshing floor. When David approached him to buy the place, Araurnah said, "No my king. I will gladly give this place to you, as well as the oxen for the sacrifice, and anything else you might need. There is no need for you to pay anything,

David's response was profound. "No I will pay, because I wouldn't think of offering to God a sacrifice that cost me nothing." A sacrifice by definition is hard, it's costly, otherwise it wouldn't be a sacrifice. I have a friend who routinely borrows money for his offerings at church, and he seldom pays it back. So who is actually making the sacrifice?

Don't run from the hard thing. Embrace it! Giving up and going back is easy. Don't give in to the easy way out. Oswald Chambers, an early 20th century Scottish evangelist once said, "Beware of going back to what you once were when God wants you to be something you have never been." Press in to receive all the treasure you can get. People who do hard things believe in miracles, they believe in the reward giver! They believe they can be something they have never been.

https://en.m.wikipedia.org/wiki/Frank_Abagnale

Chapter 5
Betrayed

He sat in his tent, rocking back and forth. Over and over he said, "Bless the Lord, oh my soul. Bless the Lord, oh my soul. Did you hear me soul? I said bless the Lord." On and on, like some kind of refrain, he continued until the fear that threatened to paralyze him dissipated. "Oh my God, I worship you. You are my strength. You are with me. I have nothing to fear."

It had been just a few short hours since he and his men had returned home, only to see everything gone and what was left burnt to the ground. He was alone and afraid, but grateful for his tent. All the others had left theirs behind as they had gone out to fight, but he had carried his with him to and from the battle, knowing he might need his should he want to be alone to pray. His men were so angry at losing their possessions and family members that they had turned on him. Now there was talk of killing him. Blamed for something David didn't do, he scurried to his hiding place. "Bless the Lord, oh my soul. Bless the Lord, oh my soul."

1 Samuel 30:6

And David was greatly distressed; for the people spake of stoning him, because the soul of all the people was grieved, every man for his sons and for his daughters: but David strengthened himself in Jehovah his God. ASV

Betrayal wounds one deeply because it speaks of broken trust, rejected love, and the feelings that come when you feel all alone in the world. David was no stranger to the darkness of betrayal. King Saul had received him, loved him, hated him, and sought to kill him all in one giant betrayal package. The darkness of this relationship was not one David wanted any part of, but he had to stay because he loved his king. He refused to betray King Saul in return, and no one could convince him to do otherwise. No, he preferred to be the one who lived in the darkness caused by the King's hatred. Instead, he choose to seek for his treasure in the darkness that surrounded him.

David understood that if he were to survive this process, he had to tell his soul what to do. He couldn't change the King, but he could change himself. No one could say David hadn't tried to restore his relationship with Saul, and yet day after day there was no relief. David ran and hid, hoping Saul would change his mind and open his heart once again to him. But it was so hard, and he was becoming weary of living in the shadows of the darkness.

Those living in Zicklag were all like David, escaping the clutches of the king. They were the poor, in debt, broken, and wanted men. There was a fear that some who came were still loyal to the king, only joining David's group to betray them all. No one knew exactly which side everyone was on. It took faith and trust to walk-in that darkness. One thing that was sure, David loved them all, no matter who they were loyal to. That was why it was so hard when his men threatened to kill him in Zicklag. David had taken them all in and provided for them without question. Now those same men threatened his life.

The pain of loving someone who has turned their back on you is beyond words, as that pain goes into the deepest parts of your soul. The darkness threatens to consume a person until there is no life left, and all David knew to do was to encourage himself in the Lord. Singing his songs of praise, he dug his way out of the darkness, finding treasure as he went. "The Lord is my light. The Lord God Almighty keeps me in the face of my enemies. He is my salvation. When people come to seek my life, it is my God who defends me."

Psalm 27:1-6
The LORD is my light and my salvation; whom shall I fear? the LORD is the strength of my life; of whom shall I be afraid?
When the wicked, even mine enemies and my foes, came upon me to eat up my flesh, they stumbled and fell.
Though an host should encamp against me, my heart shall not fear: though war should rise against me, in this will I be confident.
One thing have I desired of the LORD, that will I seek after; that I may dwell in the house of the LORD all the days of my life, to behold the beauty of the LORD, and to enquire in his temple.

For in the time of trouble he shall hide me in his pavilion:
in the secret of his tabernacle shall he hide me; he shall set
me up upon a rock.
And now shall mine head be lifted up above mine enemies
round about me: therefore will I offer in his tabernacle
sacrifices of joy; I will sing, yea, I will sing praises unto the
LORD. AV

There were treasures that David didn't know he was
unearthing with his praise. While David was encouraging
himself in the Lord, God was making him the king. King
Saul was at that same time, fighting a battle in which he
would not survive. Soon David's treasure was much
greater than he could ever imagine, for the entire kingdom
was about to become his. Not only that, but the treasures
David found, he left behind for us. He never knew that
thousands of years later, he would share his treasure of
Psalms with us. Finding God as his refuge was a treasure
that we might never know if David had not told his soul
what to do, and in doing so, taught us how to dig as well.

Psalm 62:1-8
My soul waiteth in silence for God only: From him
cometh my salvation.
He only is my rock and my salvation: He is my high tower;
I shall not be greatly moved.
How long will ye set upon a man, That ye may slay him, all
of you, Like a leaning wall, like a tottering fence?
They only consult to thrust him down from his dignity; They
delight in lies; They bless with their mouth, but they curse
inwardly. Selah
My soul, wait thou in silence for God only; For my
expectation is from him.

He only is my rock and my salvation: He is my high tower;
I shall not be moved.
With God is my salvation and my glory: The rock of my
strength, and my refuge, is in God.
Trust in him at all times, ye people; Pour out your heart
before him: God is a refuge for us. Selah ASV

Sometimes betrayal takes us by surprise. Imagine waking up from your wedding night and seeing someone you didn't expect, sleeping in your bed. That happened to Jacob. Jacob had betrayed his brother, Esau, by tricking him out of his inheritance and at the urging of his mother, he fled to her brother Laban's house. When he arrived, he fell in love at first sight with Laban's beautiful daughter, Rachel. He couldn't keep his eyes off from her, and vowed he would do anything to get her. The seven years of servitude her father demanded for her hand in marriage seemed small to him, and the days flew by, but when he woke up the morning after his wedding, it wasn't Rachel laying beside him but her older, not so pretty sister, Leah. Angry at the betrayal, he stormed into Laban's tent and demanded an answer for his trickery.

"Why did you do this to me? We had a deal. I agreed to work for seven years, and in return you promised to give me Rachel. How could you do such a thing?" Raging with anger, his face turning red as he shook his fist at his new father-in-law.

"Calm down, calm down." Laban said. "It isn't right that the younger sister marries before the oldest. Give Leah your attention for a week and then I will give you Rachel."

With a lecherous look in his eyes, he added, "Of course, you will work for me for another seven years."

Genesis 29:15-18
And Laban said unto Jacob, Because thou art my brother, shouldest thou therefore serve me for nought? tell me, what shall thy wages be?
And Laban had two daughters: the name of the elder was Leah, and the name of the younger was Rachel.
Leah was tender eyed; but Rachel was beautiful and well favoured.
And Jacob loved Rachel; and said, I will serve thee seven years for Rachel thy younger daughter.AV

The essence of betrayal is personal, and this was about as personal as it could be. Switching his daughters on Jacob's wedding night would have been a betrayal that many would not endure yet Jacob stayed. He had found a treasure he intended to get, and he wasn't about to leave without her.

His conniving father-in-law changed his wages ten times - changed the rules of their agreement over and over until Jacob had enough. Laban was even more twisted than Jacob. Looking at him, Jacob saw his own reflection, and he didn't like what he saw. His mind went back to the days he had betrayed his own brother Esau, taking his birthright and his blessing. Now he saw that he too had been evil, cut from the same cloth as his mother's brother, a deceitful, conniving fool.

Genesis 31:6-7
And ye know that with all my power I have served your father.

And your father hath deceived me, and changed my wages
ten times; but God suffered him not to hurt me. ASV

One day, God spoke to Jacob to leave and to go back to his
father's land. He was more than ready to go. The darkness
of deceit had shown him one thing. If he were to get the
fullness of his treasure, he had to go home. But going
home would not be easy. Esau was there - the one he had
betrayed.

On the way, he encountered a group of angels sent from
God to protect him as he went and then the Angel of the
Lord, God himself, came and Jacob wrestled with him all
night. He had been fighting personal demons his whole
life, but now he fought something greater than he
imagined. Hanging on for dear life he fought, never tiring,
but with an almost supernatural tenacity he hung on even
after The Lord demanded to be let go. Jacob was digging
for his treasure. He wanted to be changed. He wanted to
leave the life of betrayal behind him and was ready to
become a new man. "I won't let you go until you bless
me," He said. With a supernatural grasp, Jacob hung on,
demanding his treasure. "Bless me. Change me. I can not
leave this darkness until I am no longer the same."

Genesis 32:1-2
And Jacob went on his way, and the angels of God met
him.
And when Jacob saw them, he said, This is God's host: and
he called the name of that place Mahanaim. AV.

Genesis 32:24-30

And Jacob was left alone; and there wrestled a man with him until the breaking of the day.

And when he saw that he prevailed not against him, he touched the hollow of his thigh; and the hollow of Jacob's thigh was out of joint, as he wrestled with him.

And he said, Let me go, for the day breaketh. And he said, I will not let thee go, except thou bless me.

And he said unto him, What is thy name? And he said, Jacob.

And he said, Thy name shall be called no more Jacob, but Israel: for as a prince hast thou power with God and with men, and hast prevailed.

And Jacob asked him, and said, Tell me, I pray thee, thy name. And he said, Wherefore is it that thou dost ask after my name? And he blessed him there.

And Jacob called the name of the place Peniel: for I have seen God face to face, and my life is preserved. ASV

Jacob was digging for his treasure with all of his strength, holding on until it came. "You are no longer Jacob." The Lord said. "Now you are Israel, for you have wrestled with God and have come out with your treasure. You will never be the same."

It's an awful feeling to love, trust, or respect someone, and then to have that person turn on you. Perhaps you have been betrayed. There are fathers and mothers, husbands and wives, brothers and sisters, friends, and even some in church leadership who are guilty of betrayal for the sake of money, fame, addiction, and a host of other selfish reasons. The darkness that consumes one who has been betrayed is overwhelming, but the way out of the pit of betrayal remains the same for us today as it did for Jacob. "Oh God, don't let me become like them. Change me. I won't let you go till that happens, and I refuse to leave this dark and lonely place until I have to have my treasure. I can not leave without it."

James 1:2-4

My brethren, count it all joy
when ye fall into divers temptations;
Knowing this, that the trying of your faith
worketh patience.
But let patience have her perfect work, that ye may be
perfect and entire, wanting nothing. ASV

You see, one of the plans of the devil is to make us so hurt and angry by the betrayal that in our darkness, we become like the betrayer. But God, in his great mercy, has given us a way out, and, in the process, he has given us treasure. David wrote the Psalms and received the kingdom. Jacob, now Israel, came home to a brother who still loved him, and became the father of a nation named after him.

Just imagine what treasure you will carry out of the darkness of betrayal. James tells us we should count it all joy when we are struggling and that the treasure we find will produce strength and endurance. He tells us we will walk out of our darkness perfect and complete, wanting nothing. Oh dear friend, don't let the darkness consume you, but use the darkness as your opportunity to dig for hidden treasure. Don't let go of God until he blesses you, because you never know what glorious treasures you might find.

Chapter 6
The Victim

"Everyone gather round, and listen to me. We have to hurry as I don't know how much time we have. I just found out that the men who have protected our fields from robbers and wild animals, the ones who have been protecting us all year long, came to visit my husband this morning. They asked to be included in our harvest celebration. After all, there would not be a harvest if it hadn't been for their effort keeping us safe all year. They were only asking what was normal and acceptable, but you know my husband. He yelled at them, cursed them, and sent them away empty-handed."

"I know their commander, David, will round up his men to attack in response to my husband's folly. Hurry! We must load the donkeys with everything we can. I want two hundred loafs of bread, cakes of raisins, figs, and wineskins full of wine, five dressed sheep and some parched corn. We need to meet David on his way before he gets here, and we are all killed." The servants did as Abigail said, and soon their donkeys were laden down with their bundles.

Abigail was right. David was coming to wage war with Nabal, her husband. She met him on the road, and jumping down from her donkey, she bowled low before the future king.

1 Samuel 25:3
Now the name of the man was Nabal; and the name of his
wife Abigail: and she was a woman of good understanding,
and of a beautiful countenance: but the man was churlish
and evil in his doings; and he was of the house of Caleb.
ASV

1 Samuel 25:28-31
I pray thee, forgive the trespass of thine handmaid: for the
LORD will certainly make my lord a sure house; because
my lord fighteth the battles of the LORD, and evil hath not
been found in thee all thy days.
Yet a man is risen to pursue thee, and to seek thy soul: but
the soul of my lord shall be bound in the bundle of life with
the LORD thy God; and the souls of thine enemies, them
shall he sling out, as out of the middle of a sling.
And it shall come to pass, when the LORD shall have done
to my lord according to all the good that he hath spoken
concerning thee, and shall have appointed thee ruler over
Israel; That this shall be no grief unto thee, nor offence of
heart unto my lord, either that thou hast shed blood
causeless, or that my lord hath avenged himself: but when
the LORD shall have dealt well with my lord, then
remember thine handmaid. ASV

David looked at the woman and saw great wisdom in her.
He answered, "You are right. I was coming to kill every
male in your household. But you have been wise and come
just in time."

Abigale had a prophetic gift working inside of her. She
knew David would someday be the king, and understood

the situation perfectly, and because of her faith and courage; she saved her family from destruction.

The next morning when she told her husband what had happened, his heart failed and a few days later, he died. It wasn't long before David heard Abigail was now a widow and sent word to her she should come and be his wife.

Nabal was a fool. He was unkind and mean to everyone. Historians say that Nabal was a cruel and difficult man. Undoubtedly he abused His wife, both physically and emotionally, however she refused to become a victim in her own home. She took every opportunity to dig for treasure and found wisdom and a prophetic gift. Her faithfulness in this situation saved not only her, but her entire household. And then she eventually became the wife of David. She was not a victim of her circumstances, no she was a fighter who refused to allow her situation to dictate her future. Abigail was a treasure hunter.

Genesis 16:7-11
And the angel of the LORD found her by a fountain of water in the wilderness, by the fountain in the way to Shur. And he said, Hagar, Sarai's maid, whence camest thou? and whither wilt thou go? And she said, I flee from the face of my mistress Sarai.
And the angel of the LORD said unto her, Return to thy mistress, and submit thyself under her hands.
And the angel of the LORD said unto her, I will multiply thy seed exceedingly, that it shall not be numbered for multitude.

*And the angel of the LORD said unto her, Behold, thou art
with child, and shalt bear a son, and shalt call his name
Ishmael; because the LORD hath heard thy affliction. ASV*

Hagar was the servant of Sarai, the wife of Abram (later
known as Abraham and Sarah). God made a promise to
Abram that he would have a son and yet Sarai was barren.
One day Sarai had an idea, "Sleep with my servant Hagar
and perhaps you could have a son from her." However, as
soon as Hagar was pregnant, Sarai hated her and began
abusing her.

"Hagar, come back here. Did you hear me? Come back,
you worthless piece of scum. I won't put up with your
insolence any longer," Sarai said, while running after the
young woman. She had a broom in one hand and a rock in
the other. Throwing the rock, she narrowly missed Hagar's
head, but caught her feet with the broom. Hagar's swollen
pregnant body landed on the ground with a thud. She
couldn't live like this. The abuse from her mistress was
getting worse by the day. "How many more times can I
be beaten before I lose this baby?" Hagar wondered. When
she couldn't take it any longer, she ran away.

While she was off alone, despairing of her life, God spoke
to her and said. "I see you." Amid her darkness, God saw
her. "Go back to Sarai. I'll take care of you. Don't fear
for the child's life. He will become a great man." Clinging
to her treasure of God's promises, she returned to the house
of Abram. Hagar heard the voice of God. Knowing that
God was with her, and his kind words about the child
became her treasure, and her reason for living.

Abuse takes on many shapes, verbal, physical, financial, and emotional. Each abused person suffers in his or her own way. Some people stay in the abuse and others leave, but one thing that remains the same is the dark pit of depression and suicidal thoughts that seem to come to the victims. In a twisted way, the devil whispers to each one, "It's your fault, you know. If you hadn't done this, if you hadn't done that, these things would have never happened. It's your fault… it's your fault. You deserved what you got, and now your life is over. No one wants you. You are broken and worthless, without hope and a future." Over and over, the whispers are the same. And yet they are far from the truth.

The thing about the darkness of abuse is that you must someday come out of the darkness. If not, it will consume you. Many people who enter the darkness after being abused find comfort in the darkness of grief. They never dig for treasure, feeling they don't deserve any pleasure or happiness in life, hiding in the dark places, and never comeing out.

If you have been assaulted, raped, abused, don't give your assailant even one more day of your life by allowing him to destroy your future. No one has the right to steal your tomorrows. Elizabeth Smart, the young woman who was kidnapped in 2002, from her home and kept as a sex slave for nine months, expressed it well. "Nobody is trial-free, but we have a choice. We can choose to allow our experiences to hold us back, and to not allow us to become great or achieve greatness in this life. Or we can allow our experiences to push us forward, to make us grateful for everyday we have and to be all the more thankful for those who are around us." Elizabeth obviously found treasure in her dark places. And she had help discovering her treasure. Her mom said this to her soon after she was rescued, "Elizabeth, what this man has done to you is terrible, and there aren't words to describe how wicked and evil he is. He has taken nine months of your life that you will never get back, but don't give him another moment. The best punishment you could ever give him is to be happy."

Every time I read the story of Tamar, the beautiful daughter of King David, my heart breaks for her. She was raped by her brother, Amon. He had devised an elaborate plan to trick her into his bedroom, pretending he was sick. When she came at his request to prepare him some food, he pulled her to his bed and raped her. When he was finished with her, he threw her out like an old shirt he no longer cared for.

"Don't do this to me," she cried. "Ask, father. Surely he will give me to you as a wife." But Amon wouldn't listen and pushed her away. She went running from his room, crying and ripping her clothes. Tamar never found treasure and never came out of the darkness. The Bible says she remained in the darkness of her brother's house, lost in the despair of rape and incest, a broken, and desolate woman for her entire life.

2 Samuel 13:8-20
And when she had brought them unto him to eat, he took hold of her, and said unto her, Come lie with me, my sister. And she answered him, Nay, my brother, do not force me;

for no such thing ought to be done in Israel: do not thou this folly.

And I, whither shall I cause my shame to go? and as for thee, thou shalt be as one of the fools in Israel. Now therefore, I pray thee, speak unto the king; for he will not withhold me from thee.

Howbeit he would not hearken unto her voice: but, being stronger than she, forced her, and lay with her.

Then Amnon hated her exceedingly; so that the hatred wherewith he hated her was greater than the love wherewith he had loved her. And Amnon said unto her, Arise, be gone.

And she said unto him, There is no cause: this evil in sending me away is greater than the other that thou didst unto me. But he would not hearken unto her.

Then he called his servant that ministered unto him, and said, Put now this woman out from me, and bolt the door after her.

And she had a garment of divers colours upon her: for with such robes were the king's daughters that were virgins apparelled. Then his servant brought her out, and bolted the door after her.

And Tamar put ashes on her head, and rent her garment of divers colours that was on her, and laid her hand on her head, and went on crying.

And Absalom her brother said unto her, Hath Amnon thy brother been with thee? but hold now thy peace, my sister: he is thy brother; regard not this thing. So Tamar remained desolate in her brother Absalom's house.AV

There are many successful people who dig their way out of the darkness of severe abuse. It isn't easy, but they shovel their way out of the muck one step at a time. Depression and fear often pull them back now and then, but they persevere, still gaining ground with each step. Others struggle to let go of the past, thinking that the offended doesn't deserve forgiveness. So they hang onto every painful feeling, thinking that if they forgive or release their abuser that they are letting the person get off easily, or they are betraying the reality of their feelings, when in fact the act of unforgiveness chains them deeper into the abyss reliving the event over and over. They never understand that forgiveness is for the victim, not the offender, and unforgiveness only hurts the person who doesn't forgive.

I have a friend that I met in Bible school. Her name is Sharon. She was broken and snared by the pain of abuse in her home. When I met her, she was sad and lifeless. Her eyes looked hollow with hopelessness, and she didn't make very many friends. I often asked her about her family, but she wouldn't tell me anything until I insisted. Her reply stunned me. "My family smells like death."

One week at Bible school, we had a guest speaker who taught on forgiveness. God spoke to Sharon about going home and talking to her stepfather. The Lord told her she needed to apologize for anything she might have done to make her stepfather's life difficult and also to forgive him. He had been very cruel to her, and she had spent many nights filled with nightmares, reliving the abuse she suffered.

She didn't want to go and told the Lord, "I can't go home. I have no way to get there and the distance is far."

It wasn't long before another student stopped by her room and said, "I just found out we live close to each other. I'm going home this weekend. Would you like to go?"

Stunned that God had made a way for her to go home so quickly, she said yes."

When she arrived home, she found out her stepfather was dying, and wouldn't live long. As a matter of fact, she was one of the last to speak to him before he died. She apologized and asked for his forgiveness, and he railed at her like he always did, but she said nothing in return and forgave him in her heart. When she returned to school, I noticed a big difference in Sharon. She smiled a lot. The emptiness was gone, and she made a lot of friends. The change was obvious and profound.

We stayed in touch through the years and I taught on the power of forgiveness and inner healing with my ladies' group at church. I told them Sharon's story. We had a wonderful time where several of the ladies responded to the message and it changed their lives. I went home and called my friend. "Sharon, you won't believe what the Lord did today. I shared your story with my ladies' group and several were powerfully impacted with your story."

"What story?" She asked.

I said, "You know about how you suffered growing up, and how difficult it was for you." I reminded her of the speaker at Bible school and her trip home and how when she returned, she was a different person.

She told me she didn't know what I was talking about, that she never suffered. I was stunned and said, yes you did. I told her all the stories she had told me about her family and when I finished, she said, "I forgot. I forgot! I FORGOT! Can you believe it? I forgot. It's like a movie I saw, or a book that I read. That past isn't mine anymore."

Perhaps you have been abused. Spend a minute and talk to the Lord. Tell Him you forgive your abuser and ask him to free you from your past. Freedom is a treasure that can be had for anyone who will dig their way out of their past. Don't say in your heart that God can't set you free, because if he did it for one person, He can do it for many!

People who refuse to forgive, often struggle with fear, and remain a captive of their abuser long after the abuse has ended. They don't find treasure because they don't believe there is any to be found. And evil spirits trap them even deeper, telling them that the darkness is safe. But treasures abound for those who risk leaving the darkness. There are those who find the treasure of forgiveness, and slowly dig their way out of the despair, and pick up other golden nuggets such as peace, hope, a new past, and a bright future on their way out.

Jeremiah 29:11

For I know the thoughts that I think toward you, saith the LORD, thoughts of peace, and not of evil, to give you an expected end. ASV

Dear friend. If this is your story, don't be like Tamar, and live in your brokenness. Take the risk and venture into the world of redemption, hope, and forgiveness, gathering up all the courage and treasures you can find.   Sharon, Abigail, Hagar, and Elizabeth Smart walked out of their despair, and you can too.

https://www.ksl.com/article/19942794/elizabeth-smart-the-best-punishment-i-could-give-him-is-to-be-happ

Chapter 7
Never Alone

I had only been driving a few months when my dad told me to go to the store and pick up a few things. My grandparents were visiting and my mom needed a few groceries. It never occurred to me to check the gas gage (a problem I still have today), and on the way home the car ran out of gas. I could get the car onto the shoulder of the road as it sputtered to a stop, and so I just rolled up the windows, locked the doors, leaned my seat back, closed my eyes, and waited. I knew my dad would come looking for me.

Of course, I didn't come home when my dad expected me, so he and my grandfather came looking for me. As they drove, my grandfather saw the car on the side of the road. "Hay, look there. Isn't that your car?"

Sure enough, it was. They pulled my grandfather's car up behind me and my dad walked over to the car and tapped on the window. I must have been asleep, as his tap startled me. I rolled down the window, and he said, "What are you doing?"

I said, "Waiting for you. I knew you would come." And sure enough, he had. Any time I needed him, he was always there, especially if he thought I might have to do something alone. "You don't want to do that alone. I'll go with you."

Fred could not stay with me on my first night in the Roswell Cancer hospital, so my dad stayed that night in my hospital room with me. I was thirty-eight years old, yet my daddy sat all night, with his hand on my foot, or holding my hand, praying for me.

Only a few months later, Fred and I flew to Vladivostok, Russia. When we arrived, the pastor asked Fred to help him with some computer issues. I knew this could take a long time, and it had been a long journey. I was exhausted, and all I wanted to do was to go to bed. We had been shown where we were to be staying at the Bible school, and I asked if I could be taken there so that I could sleep. The pastor said yes, and took me out to the abandoned army camp where the Bible school and our bedroom were located, a few miles from town. Both Fred and the pastor assured me it wouldn't be long and the pastor would return with Fred.

I fell asleep quickly and woke up around 8pm. Fred and the pastor hadn't returned yet, so I went back to sleep. I woke again about 10:30pm, midnight, and 2am. Still no pastor and no Fred. I didn't have a phone, nor could I speak any Russian. By 6am the students were all fixing breakfast and with various hand signals, they let me know I should join them. At 8am, the students and I were assembled in one of the makeshift classrooms for the first class of the day, but no pastor, no translator, and no Fred. Finally, around 8:30, they showed up.

Fred was very upset and full of apologies. He had fully expected to meet me at the Bible school, but when they got done with all the computer work, about midnight, the pastor informed him that all the streets were closed and it was forbidden to drive that time of night. So Fred would have to wait until morning, while I was left to spend my first night in Russia alone.

While some people may have panicked. I was in perfect peace. Not even once was I afraid. I learned years ago when I ran out of gas, when I had to go some place alone, when I was dealing with cancer that I was never really alone. Daddy had always been there for me. And that was how I felt my first night alone in Russia. I knew my Heavenly Daddy would always be there for me, no matter where in the world I was. Without even realizing it, I had drawn on the treasure I had found years ago on the side of the road.

Fred has done the same for our daughter, Marie-Louise. Soon after we adopted her, there was a powerful rainstorm, and Fred jumped out of our bed. I was startled and asked him what he was doing.

"It's raining really hard right now and I know if it thunders with lightning, Marie-Louise will be afraid."

Just as he got to her bedroom door, the lightning flashed bright preceded by a loud resounding boom. Marie-Louise sat bolt upright screaming, "Daddy, where are you?"

His reply? "I was here before you called." That moment became her treasure in dark places.

Isaiah 65:24
Before they call I will answer; while they are yet speaking I will hear. AV

It must have been that way for Samuel when he was just a scared little boy, left to stay with Eli, the priest. I can't imagine what it was like for him to be separated from his mom and dad at such a young age, and yet he learned to hear God's voice and knew that his Abba (Daddy) Father was always with him, a treasure he found and drew strength from his entire life.

"We want a king. We want to be like everyone else." Just the words were heartbreaking to Samuel. He was always strong and seldom disrespected, but on that day he felt utter rejection, and shook inside from a broken heart. For the first time in his life, I imagine he felt completely alone. No one stood up for the beloved prophet that day.

"I have never cheated you or harmed you, or done anything but bless you, and now you want a king. You don't understand, the king will take your sons and send them to war. I have never sent anyone to war. He will require you to pay taxes, and make you his servants, something I have never done. That's what kings do." He might as well have been talking to a stone wall for all the good it did. No one wanted to listen to the old prophet. He felt shaken, beaten, and completely alone. Except he wasn't. God was there. He was Samuel's treasure that day.

"Samuel, why are you feeling so bad about this king situation?" God asked. "They haven't rejected you, they rejected me!"

1 Samuel 8:7
And the LORD said unto Samuel, Hearken unto the voice of the people in all that they say unto thee: for they have not rejected thee, but they have rejected me, that I should not reign over them. AV

Can you imagine God being rejected? Can you imagine how that must have felt to God? And yet it was a lonely and solitary rejection that Jesus bore on the cross for you and me.

The night was dark, and the moon was hanging high in the sky, while his three friends leaned against a tree sound asleep. As his friends slept through his lonely anguish, he could hear Peter snoring. He knew what he was about to do and saw the cross as he knelt there that night. He saw the moment when the sky turned black and the earth shook. Yes, he saw it all as he prayed that night, all alone. You see, Jesus purchased treasures that night for you and for me. He suffered and carried all the burdens alone, so you and I don't have to. Crying in the garden, he prayed alone. He stood before Pilate alone, faced his accusers, was spit upon and ridiculed, alone. Without a friend to plead his case, he suffered alone, so we would never be alone.

It must've been a bittersweet moment as he remembered the prayer that he taught his disciples to pray, "Our Father, who is in heaven, holy is your name. Let your kingdom

come, and your will be done in earth as it is in heaven. Oh
Father, if it is at all possible, deliver me from this situation.
Nevertheless, not as I choose, but as you will. Let it be
done here on earth as it has been done in heaven. Oh
Father, don't let me fail and give into temptation, but give
me the strength, my daily bread, to sustain me on this
journey and not give in to evil. Work out your merciful
forgiveness and redemption in my life. This is all for your
eternal kingdom, your miraculous power, and the wonder
of your glorious majesty. Oh Father, holy holy is your
name…". Over and over he prayed, all alone, for you and
for me.

Luke 11:2-4
*And he said unto them, When ye pray, say, Our Father
which art in heaven, Hallowed be thy name. Thy kingdom
come. Thy will be done, as in heaven, so in earth.
Give us day by day our daily bread.
And forgive us our sins; for we also forgive every one that
is indebted to us. And lead us not into temptation; but
deliver us from evil. AV*

Matthew 6:9-13
*"…thus therefore pray ye: 'Our Father who art in the
heavens! hallowed be Thy name.
'Thy reign come: Thy will come to pass, as in heaven also
on the earth.
'Our appointed bread give us to-day.
'And forgive us our debts, as also we forgive our debtors.
'And mayest Thou not lead us to temptation, but deliver us
from the evil, because Thine is the reign, and the power,
and the glory — to the ages. Amen." YLT*

I don't think there is anything more difficult to live with than the feeling of being rejected, and not wanted, alone. Of course, that is exactly how Jesus felt as he hung on the cross. During one of his agonizing breaths he cried out, "My God, my God, why have you forsaken me," He knew when he went to the cross that he would carry the sin of the world on his body, and that the Holy Father could not look on him when that happened. But that didn't change the fact that Jesus, the Son of God and the Son of man, felt the anguish of being alone.

Matthew 27:46
And about the ninth hour Jesus cried with a loud voice, saying, Eli, Eli, lama sabachthani? that is to say, My God, my God, why hast thou forsaken me? AV

Jesus suffered in the garden of Gethsemane. In agony, he sweat drops of blood as he prayed the night before his crucifixion. Then the Bible says he went to the dark places of hell to break the stronghold of death, so that he could purchase our treasured redemption. He came, having left everything behind, having left all of heaven and its glory, he entered this world of sin and death alone. He willingly went through dark places and suffered alone, in order to receive the treasure that he freely gives to you and me.

Hebrews 5:7-9
Who in the days of his flesh, having offered up prayers and supplications with strong crying and tears unto him that was able to save him from death, and having been heard for his godly fear,
though he was a Son, yet learned obedience by the things which he suffered;

and having been made perfect, he became unto all them
that obey him the author of eternal salvation… ASV

Dear friend, if you feel alone, you have a Heavenly Father who is always with you. Just like my dad, he is holding your hand and staying close, comforting you in your troubles. You are never alone. Jesus paid the ultimate price for the wonderful treasure of God's presence. He suffered alone, so you don't have to.

Chapter 8

The Best Day

I found a book in the library during one of their annual book sales. It was the story of Shadrach, Meshak, and Abednigo, complete with colorful pictures, written word for word out of the King James version of the Bible. It became our son's favorite bedtime story, and every night, before he would go to sleep, he would say, "Read the story of the Fiery Furnace again."

Nebuchadnezzar, the king, erected an enormous golden image. He declared that whenever there would be the sound of the horn, pipe, lyre, trigon, harp, bagpipe, and every kind of music, that everyone must bow down and worship the golden image. Some people believe it was an image of Nebuchadnezzar himself and that he wanted people to worship his image declaring him to be God. It sure sounds like something this evil, proud king would do.

There were people who hated Shadrach, Meshak, and Abednigo. So they went and told king Nebuchadnezzar. "There are some Israelites here who don't believe the way we do. They're foreigners. You said that if someone doesn't worship the golden image that you have built, then they would be thrown into a fiery furnace. Well, oh King,

Shadrach, Meshak, and Abednigo refuse to bow before your golden image."

So the king called the three young men and asked, "I hear you won't bow down and worship my golden image? Is that true? I will give you another chance. If you will worship now, you'll be saved, but if you don't bow down and worship my image, then you're going to be thrown into the fiery furnace."

Our young heroes answered, "We really don't need to talk to you about this. If you want to throw us into the furnace, that is fine, because we refuse to bow before your idol. We are not afraid or concerned. God can deliver us from you or the furnace. Either way, we won't bow down to your image."

Daniel 3:16-18
Shadrach, Meshach, and Abed-nego answered and said to the king, O Nebuchadnezzar, we have no need to answer thee in this matter.
If it be so, our God whom we serve is able to deliver us from the burning fiery furnace; and he will deliver us out of thy hand, O king.
But if not, be it known unto thee, O king, that we will not serve thy gods, nor worship the golden image which thou hast set up. ASV

Well, Nebuchadnezzar's face changed from that of a benevolent monarch, giving Shadrach, Meshak, and Abednigo another chance, to that of an angry, arrogant king. He sent word to heat the furnace seven times hotter. He demanded that Shadrach, Meshak, and Abednigo to be bound with their hats, coats, and everything they were wearing, and then be thrown into the fire. It was so hot that the men who threw Shadrach, Meshak, and Abednigo into the furnace died.

As the king was watching, he saw people walking in the fire. He asked to those watching with him, "Didn't we send three into the fire? I see four and the fourth one looks like the Son of God."

God had burned off the ropes bound around Shadrach, Meshak, and Abednigo, and they were walking inside of that fiery furnace with the son of God.

Imagine what it was like for Shadrach when he became an old man, gathering together all of his grandchildre. "Come children. I want to tell you about the best day of my life. It was the day I walked with God, hand in hand, face to face."

When it looked like everything was lost for Shadrach, Meshak, and Abednigo, Jesus was with them. That day, walking in the fire became the best day of their lives. Those three walked with God and when the king saw them, he ordered them to come out of the fire. The ropes that had been bound around them were burnt off, but their bodies were not burned. None of their clothes were scorched, nor did they smell of smoke. They were completely delivered.

There is no other wound that is any more painful than a burn, and there's nothing more terrifying than burning up in a fire. Yet when Shadrach, Meshak, and Abednigo. were sent into that fiery furnace, they realized God was with them and His fire was much greater than that of the furnace. They found a treasure. Not only did they find a treasure, but they provided treasure for the king and for the people of the land, as when they came out of their trial, they were promoted and taught the people about their God. Yes indeed it was the best day of their lives."

One of the greatest treasures we will ever find is faith, faith that believes even in the face of death. Faith will always be tried in order to become stronger. Earlier in this book, I tell the story of cancer, and how my faith was offended. But like Shadrach, Meshak, and Abednigo, I took a stand and did not allow my circumstances to dictate to me where I would place my faith. When I told the Lord that I would not leave him, whether or not he healed me. He then told me I had faith. Remember, faith is not faith unless it has been tried. It has not been tried until it has been offended and still believes. The trying of our faith is necessary to develop mature faith, as it brings our faith to a whole new level. I didn't understand what it meant to have my faith offended and yet in my trial, during some of the darkest days of my life, God told me I had faith. I found a treasure in my dark place, a treasure I wasn't even expecting or looking for. This treasure opened up areas of the Word of God that I had never understood. In the same way, Shadrach, Meshak, and Abednigo went through their dark faith-trying situation, and they remained strong. Faith became their treasure, and the day they found it was the best day of their lives.

~~~~

He yawned and rolled over, snuggling deep into the fur. The sun wasn't up yet, and between the darkness and the rhythmic purring of the cat, he didn't feel like waking up yet. A few hours later, he woke with a start as he heard someone calling his name. "Daniel! Daniel! Has your God delivered you from the lions?"

Lifting the heavy paw draped around his shoulders, Daniel sat up and rubbed his eyes. He couldn't shake the feeling that he had just had the best night's sleep that he'd ever had in his whole life.

King Darius favored Daniel and made plans to put Danial in charge of the entire kingdom. Of course, that didn't set well with some of the other influential people of the day. Jealous, they devised a plan to get rid of him. Who was this Daniel, anyway? He was a foreigner, a Hebrew. He wasn't one of them, but Daniel was honorable in everything he did and was very close to the king. Soon, they realized the only way to get rid of him was to use his relationship with God against him.

Daniel 6:5
Then said these men, We shall not find any occasion against this Daniel, except we find it against him concerning the law of his God. ASV

They went to the king and suggested a new law, a law that demanded that no one could ask or pray for anything from anyone or any god except the King, for thirty days. If anyone should break this law, they would be thrown into a den of hungry lions. King Darius liked the sound of such a decree. It would make him higher than any god, at least for thirty days. So he quickly agreed and established the proclamation according to the laws of the Medes and the

Persians, and a law established in this way could never be broken.

When Daniel heard about the law, he ignored it. He had no intention of changing his prayer life or setting his relationship with the Lord on hold for thirty days. So he went to his room, opened his window and prayed like he did every day.

His enemies, who had been waiting in the shadows, knowing that he would refuse to comply with the new law, saw him and quickly reported Daniel to the king.

It was a sad day for the king. He really liked Daniel. He'd been trapped, and he sought for a way to save his friend, but he was reminded over and over again that the edict had been established according to the laws of the Medes and Persians. It could not be broken.

The king said, "Oh my friend, I hope your God can get you out of this situation. You pray to Him every day. I truly hope He can help you this night." After saying that, Daniel was thrown into the lion's den, and the king's heart was broken. Staying up all night fretting over Daniel's life, the king could hardly wait for the morning to come, so he could see if Daniel's God had saved him from certain death. He thought his heart would stop when he first looked into the den. He couldn't see his friend at first, but after calling out his name, he saw one of the lions move and out came Daniel.

"Oh yes, my King, my God shut the mouths of the lions. He kept me all night, and you know what? I think it was the best night of my life."

Daniel 6:21-22
Then said Daniel unto the king, O king, live for ever. My God hath sent his angel, and hath shut the lions' mouths, and they have not hurt me; forasmuch as before him innocency was found in me; and also before thee, O king, have I done no hurt. ASV

Can you imagine that? Of course, the Bible doesn't tell us that Daniel and the lions slept together, but we know God sent his Angel, or as in the story of Shadrach, Meshach, and Abednego, the Son of God. He came and shut the mouths of the lions.

Treasures abound in these stories. These men each had a 'one on one' encounter with God. They walked with God and talked to Him, and were not alone. The kings in these stories promoted all four men in their earthly kingdoms. Their faith was tested and proven and strengthened.

1 John 1:5
And this is the message which we have heard from him and announce unto you, that God is light, and in him is no darkness at all. ASV

Don't let your dark trials steal your faith. Everyone was submitting to the edicts of the kings, but not Daniel, Shadrach, Meshach, and Abednego. They remained true to God, even amid great persecution. They wouldn't bend or bow along with everyone else. Yes, those dark places are scary places to think about, but as I found out in my own life, a dark place isn't so dark when Jesus is walking through it with you. Remember, the Bible tells us that Jesus is the Light and in him is no darkness. No wonder it was easy for the king to see four men walking in the fire. No wonder the lions were calm the night Daniel slept with them. The light was there and everything must submit to the Light! What a treasure we have in our "all consuming Jesus". He makes even our darkest trials, the best days of our lives.

Chapter 9

Loss

He woke with a start. The dream had been so real he could almost taste his mother's cooking. The lentils on the stove, the roasted lamb over the open fire, and just the thought of the barley bread that she made every day made his stomach growl in anticipation. But it was just a dream, just a faraway dream. He tried to stop thinking about home. But night after night, the dreams were the same and lately they had become more real than ever before. He tried to shut them out of his memory, but he couldn't. Suddenly he understood. He needed to go home.

How long it took to come to this conclusion he didn't know. He should have realized it weeks ago. Yes, he should just go home. Every time he thought about it, his stomach tied him up in knots. What should he say when he got there? How will they react when he shows up? Surely they won't reject him. His father was a kind man. "I know," he thought. "I'll be straight with Father right from the beginning and tell him I was wrong and beg his forgiveness. At the very least, he will let me sleep in the barn."

The journey was long and the little food he had last eaten wasn't setting right with him. His stomach twisted and turned, threatening to erupt at any moment. But he pressed on reflecting on how much he had changed since he left home. His pockets had been full of money and he had splendid ideas of what he would do with it all. Arriving in the big city, he quickly made lots of friends. How was he to know that they were only his friends for as long as his money held out? He was only a country boy, trusting all the wrong people. When his money was gone, so were the friends.

With no place to stay and nothing to eat, he went to a local farmer and took a job feeding the pigs. But even the pig farmer wasn't generous. Every day, he watched those pigs eat the scraps from the farmer's table. It was rotten slop, but he coveted it. Looking at the pigs he fed while his stomach growled made him wonder what it would be like to eat their food, and then he realized how stupid that was. Who wanted to eat rotten old pig slop?

So off he went, trudging down the road he knew so well. After several hours, he stopped to take a rest. Then, as he stood to start his journey again, his head spun. He was weaker than he thought. "Maybe this is a bad idea. They won't even recognize me when I get home. I should just turn around and…"

Suddenly, a hand grabbed him by the shoulder and turned him around. Staring him in the eyes, face to face, was his dad. "I've been waiting for you, son."

"You… you've been waiting for me? Really?"

With tears in his eyes, the old man nodded his head, "Yes, every day since you left, I've been waiting for you. I have stood here by the road and waited, and waited, praying that the Almighty would bring you home safe to me." In truth, the old man had many long conversations with the Almighty, as he waited for his son to come home. "Oh Mighty God, I shouldn't have let him go. Please bring him home. What if he was robbed, or worse? He was much too young to go off on his own. What if I never see him again? How can I live with myself if I find out he has died? Oh God, what did I do?"

Both the son and the father carried the enormous load of guilt burdened with the "what ifs." But now was not the time for "what if's." It was time to celebrate.

The reception was almost too much to bear. The son was rushed away by the servants who cleaned him up and gave him a coat, a ring, and shoes for his feet, all new treasures saved just for him, for the day when he would come home. Then they killed a calf and made a feast.

Humiliated, he said, "Father, I have sinned against heaven and against you. I am not worthy to be called your son. Just let me live in the barn and be your servant."

"Nonsense! You are my son. I thought you were dead and I would never see you and again. You were lost, but I have found you. Come celebrate with me."

I have read this story many times and there is a wealth of riches that is buried deep inside of this story. Treasures that even the father and his son could not see that first day, but treasures nonetheless. The son found forgiveness, grace, understanding, not to mention all the food he could eat and a safe and comfortable bed to sleep in for the rest of his life. And the father found his child, but also love like he had never known before came from his boy because he who is forgiven much, loves much. The arrogance and cockiness that his son carried with him the day he left was gone, replaced by faithfulness and appreciation.

There are two players in this story: the son and the father, the one who leaves and the one who stays, the lost and the finder, the faithful and the unfaithful, the lover and the brokenhearted. And in the hearts and minds of these two are a bundle of emotions, confusion, hurt, shock, sadness, guilt, grief, and despair. They both suffered the trauma of their loss and the guilt that the devil always tries to overwhelm us with. But our amazing Heavenly Father always leaves behind treasure for those who are burdened with grief. It's just waiting to be found.

There are all kinds of loss. Some have lost their home in a natural disaster or because of finances. Others have lost a child or spouse to addiction. Broken families suffer from hurt feelings, lost finances, abuse, or death. None can deny that each one suffers in the darkness of loss. Their loss becomes the proverbial rug pulled out from underneath them and everything they thought was sure becomes quick sand. This is when you know you are standing on the solid rock and that this rock, Christ, is your treasure.

There is an old hymn that says, "My hope is built on nothing less than Jesus' blood and righteousness. I dare not trust the sweetest frame, but wholly lean on Jesus' name. On Christ the solid rock I stand, all other ground is sinking sand. When darkness seems to hide His face, I rest on His unchanging grace."

What a comfort it is when everything is against us, when we have lost what is most precious, when we feel like there is no hope, and when darkness seems to hide even the face of God, we know that we have something firm to stand upon, our solid rock, Christ Jesus. That is treasure indeed.

When my father was dying, I sat by his bedside every day, hoping and praying that he wouldn't die. He told me over and over that he was going to heaven, but I begged him not to go just yet. I knew it was a lost cause, but I couldn't stop myself from begging him to stay. I cried myself to sleep most of those nights after I left his hospital room. Every day, I was the first to his room before anyone else came, and I stayed until everyone else had left, keeping my watchful vigil, praying for a miracle. On the last day, when he went to heaven, I dried my tears. I couldn't explain it. I had cried for days. Now he was gone, and so were my tears.

Then I remembered the story of King David, when his baby lay dying. He cried and cried, begging God to let the child live. Then on the day the baby died. David courageously dried his tears. Everyone was shocked. They were sure David would be inconsolable, but no, he wasn't. As a matter of fact, it seemed like he didn't care, but he did. His response when people asked him why he wasn't sad was this: "He can't come to me, but I can go to him." He knew he had to live his life in such a way that he would go to heaven where his child was and they would see each other there.

2 Samuel 12:21-23
Then said his servants unto him, What thing is this that thou hast done? thou didst fast and weep for the child, while it was alive; but when the child was dead, thou didst rise and eat bread.
And he said, While the child was yet alive, I fasted and wept: for I said, Who knoweth whether Jehovah will not be gracious to me, that the child may live?

But now he is dead, wherefore should I fast? can I bring him back again? I shall go to him, but he will not return to me. ASV

I think one of the most difficult losses to bear is the loss of a child. And it is very difficult to know how to look for treasure when someone's life is cut short. Remember, our Heavenly Father knows what it feels like to lose a child. He lost his own for you and for me. He suffered the loss so we would know that we have a God who shares in our suffering.

John 3:16
For God so loved the world, that he gave his only begotten Son, that whosoever believeth on him should not perish, but have eternal life. ASV

Imagine the homecoming when David came to the end of his life, and he walked into the gates of heaven. Standing there with the Lord is the baby that died so many years before. With open arms he cries, "I've been waiting for you, dad. I have looked down the road of your life, every day, waiting for you to come home. Let me show you all the treasures you have laid up in heaven. I've been watching over them for you. Come Dad, look! We have new shoes and a robe of righteousness for you. I'm so excited because you are finally here. I have so much to show you, and so much to tell you about heaven."

Matthew 6:19-21
Lay not up for yourselves treasures upon the earth, where moth and rust consume, and where thieves break through and steal:

but lay up for yourselves treasures in heaven, where neither moth nor rust doth consume, and where thieves do not break through nor steal: for where thy treasure is, there will thy heart be also. ASV

That was how I felt when my dad died. He couldn't come to me, but I could go to him. I remember my mom asking who we should get to do the funeral/memorial service. I said, "I will do it." She looked at me and asked, "You? You are going to do your own father's funeral?"

I said, "Yes I am."

My sister added, "I'll do it with you."

We did it. My sister and I. Neither of us shed a tear or a sob. Not because we didn't care, because we cared. Not because we didn't feel the loss, because we did. But because we had dried our eyes and now, it was time to get with the business of going to see him. So we had a treasure seeking memorial. We dug deep into my dad's life, looked at pictures, and recalled memories. We laughed and sang, rejoicing in the life of my dad that God had given to us. Like David, I know my dad can't come to me, but someday I will go where he is.

The prodigal lost much when he went away, as did his father. Both felt an enormous loss. Both lived in a season of darkness as they mourned their loss. Neither was exempt in the darkness. But there was treasure there for them both. Treasures they might never have found had it not been for the dark places they traveled between when the son was lost and when he was found.

Some treasures are laid up for us in heaven, waiting for our arrival. Perhaps you have mourned a loved one for a long time. Grief has settled deep in your spirit and you feel like something is broken inside. Ask the Lord, "Do you have a treasure for me? Remind me of the good times. Give me treasured memories." Or perhaps the one you lost never knew the Lord and you fear if he or she will be in heaven. God still has treasure for you. Give your grief to the Lord. He knows how to take away the pain and replace it with his presence.

God understands how it feels to lose a loved one. He understands your grief, and he feels your pain. Even if it has been years ago since you lost someone, God knows how it feels to remember the freshness of that loss each time you think of them. He knows what it is to be alone, and that the devil torments you with thoughts of what could have been. God knows, and he is there waiting for you to discover the treasure of his presence, his peace and his love.

Don't give up, dear friend. There is treasure to be found. Dig for it. And when you find the solid rock, stand. Stand firm knowing the Lord has brought you through the valley of loss and now you stand on a treasured solid rock. Stand knowing that even when you didn't know He was there, Jesus stood with you, and you were never alone.

Matthew 7:7-11
Ask, and it shall be given you; seek, and ye shall find; knock, and it shall be opened unto you:

for every one that asketh receiveth; and he that seeketh findeth; and to him that knocketh it shall be opened. Or what man is there of you, who, if his son shall ask him for a loaf, will give him a stone; or if he shall ask for a fish, will give him a serpent? If ye then, being evil, know how to give good gifts unto your children, how much more shall your Father who is in heaven give good things to them that ask him? ASV

On Christ The Solid Rock
by Edward Mote
© Public Domain

Chapter 10
The Reason

"You have got to be kidding me. I can't believe what that man said to me.   Can you believe it? I came all the way here, and he didn't even have the common courtesy to come out and greet me.   Who does he think I am? Am I a nobody that he would send out his servant, and tell me to go take a bath in that filthy dirty river!"

"Well, I won't do it. I won't. That is the craziest thing I have ever heard. Go wash in the Jordan River. That muddy, murky river? Really! I've got a skin disease, and he wants me to go wash in that place? I'm going back to Damascus and I'll wash in the beautiful rivers there. Now that is the place to go, gardens lining the rivers that flow from the mountains with crystal clear waters. Nothing like that filthy Jordan." Having said all of that, Naaman turned away and jumped up into his chariot, ready to go home.

He had a servant who traveled with him who said, "Sir, please. What do you have to lose? You came all the way here - such a long journey. Surely it won't hurt to do as the man says. If he had demanded lots of money, you would have gladly paid. Don't you think you should try?"

So, having been persuaded by his servant, Naaman went to the Jordan river and dipped into the water, while his servant counted off the times. "Remember, Sir, the prophet said to dip seven times."

One dip, two, three, "This is the dumbest thing I have ever done. I'm going home," sputtered Naaman.

"Please, don't give up. Dip again." Fourth, Five.

"See, nothing has changed." Sixth, seven.

2 Kings 5:10-14

And Elisha sent a messenger unto him, saying, Go and wash in the Jordan seven times, and thy flesh shall come again to thee, and thou shalt be clean.
But Naaman was wroth, and went away, and said, Behold, I thought, He will surely come out to me, and stand, and call on the name of Jehovah his God, and wave his hand over the place, and recover the leper.
Are not Abanah and Pharpar, the rivers of Damascus, better than all the waters of Israel? may I not wash in them, and be clean? So he turned and went away in a rage.
And his servants came near, and spake unto him, and said, My father, if the prophet had bid thee do some great thing, wouldest thou not have done it? how much rather then, when he saith to thee, Wash, and be clean?
Then went he down, and dipped himself seven times in the Jordan, according to the saying of the man of God; and his flesh came again like unto the flesh of a little child, and he was clean. ASV

Out of the water flew the shocked commander. His body had been hit by something so powerful that it propelled him out of the water, and his stunned body landed with a thud on the ground. Trembling, and looking at his skin, his servant said, "Look Sir! Look! Your body is healed. You're healed."

Elijah told Naaman to dip in the Jordan River, the river that the Israelites crossed to get to the Promised land and later the river Jesus was baptized in. It was a river that symbolized new beginnings. I made little sense to the mighty Naaman, but not to God. This was where Naaman's treasure lay. It was the way to his promised land. And he almost missed his treasure, all because he didn't understand.

It is interesting that nothing was said about Naaman personally. Had he sinned! Had he been a cruel master? Was he innocent? Guilty? Why did he get leprosy? How did it happen that he ended up that way? No one knows. It doesn't matter, all that mattered was whether or not he would dip in the Jordan.

Many people assume that sin is the reason people suffer. While ultimately the reason for sickness, pain, and suffering is that we live in a sinful world, it has not been the primary focus of this book. All too often, good people who are suffering openly question the reason for their pain. Then well-meaning friends, in an effort to help, ask, "Is there sin in your life? Perhaps this suffering results from unconfessed sin." Then, riddled with guilt, the sufferer begins soul searching. When coming up empty-handed, their friends then shake their heads, convinced that sin is there, but the sick person doesn't want to admit it.

When Fred and I were first married, Fred went through a season when his blood sugar would drop and, as a result, he was very sick. We went from church service to church service, seeking God and looking for an answer for his suffering. We even traveled to a nearby city with friends to hear a healing evangelist. On the way, our friends suggested that there was sin involved in Fred's or my life that had caused his sickness. Then, sitting in the meeting, the evangelist took up an offering. He told everyone that their healing depended on the amount given in the offering. If you gave $100, you got a $100 healing. The same was for $50, $20, $10, or even $5. We had little money as Fred had been so sick and hadn't been able to work. We were devastated and arrived home that night in worse shape than we were earlier in the day. Now we wondered if there was some sin we didn't know about and we were sure that our small offering to the evangelist wasn't enough to get a healing.

Soon I became desperate and decided to fast and pray for Fred. I fasted for a week, knowing that the only hope we had was God. Not long after, we had a guest speaker in our church. I was sitting in the front row of the church and Fred was sitting in the sound booth in the back. I was on the edge of my seat listening to this man as he spoke. He was talking about the power of God that could heal, deliver, and set people free. I just knew in my heart that this was Fred's night.

At the end of the message, the man offered for people to come forward for prayer. He asked if anyone needed to be healed, and I turned around, hoping to catch Fred's eye. He saw me and I motioned for him to come up to the front, but he wouldn't budge. I kept signaling him, but he stopped looking at me, so I had to go down the aisle and get him. I got to the back door of the sound booth and grabbed his arm. "Come on, I said. Go up and get prayer."

He said, "No. I will not let that guy pray for me. He looks funny."

I kept pulling and half dragged him to the front. To be fair, we both had been so hurt by the last evangelist it was hard to believe again, but in my heart I knew this was Fred's night. We made quite the spectacle as we fought in the aisle all the way to the front, but I wouldn't give up.

When we got to the front. The evangelist asked Fred what it was he wanted and Fred said, "I want to be healed."

The man said, "Look at the faith this young man has! Be healed in Jesus' name." Instantly Fred was healed, and he has had no sugar regulating problems since that day.

Looking back over forty years later, I am reminded of what God showed us in that season. I have cherished in my heart the treasure that God still heals today. Money can not buy healing or favor from God. I now understand that God isn't withholding his kindness to me because of some unknown sin or because I didn't put enough money in the offering plate. Yes, there are sicknesses and problems that come because of sin, but sin or no sin, we can not become good enough to be healed. God is faithful and will show us if we have sin issues. We don't have to fear that there is some secret sin that we don't know about. He isn't shy to tell us when we need correction or rebellion, because rebellion is never a secret.

2 Corinthians 4:7-10

But we have this treasure in earthen vessels, that the
exceeding greatness of the power
may be of God, and not from ourselves;
we are pressed on every side, yet not straitened;
perplexed, yet not unto despair;
pursued, yet not forsaken; smitten down, yet not destroyed;
always bearing about in the body the dying of Jesus, that
the life also of Jesus may be manifested in our body. ASV

The Apostle Paul tells us we have treasure inside of us, and that the treasure is from God, full of His power. We may be squeezed by the world, confused by our circumstances, struggling to understand, but through it all, the life of Jesus is manifested in our bodies. And then he further explains that if the Spirit (our treasure) that raised Christ from the dead dwells in us, then that Spirit will quicken, make alive, or restore life to our earthly bodies. You see, we don't need our heavenly bodies restored. We need our earthly bodies made new.

Romans 8:11

But if the Spirit of him that raised up Jesus from the dead
dwell in you, he that raised up Christ from the dead shall
also quicken your mortal bodies by his Spirit that dwelleth
in you.AV

There was a man who had been born blind. He was found begging on the side of the road as Jesus passed by. His disciples asked him why the man had been born blind. Was it because of sin in his life or the life of his parents? It seemed they thought it was a hard fast rule. If you are sick or suffer some kind of tragedy, obviously someone sinned and caused it. But Jesus said, "Neither sinned. He was born blind, so the glory of the Lord would be shown to you."

John 9:3

Jesus answered, "Neither hath this man sinned, nor his parents: but that the works of God should be made manifest in him." AV

What a burden of guilt that man must have carried through the years with people shunning him, because they didn't want any part of his sin. For surely his sin caused him to be born blind. Sin! Before he was born? Really? But that is what they thought, and it was reflected in how he was treated. He was the scum of the earth, destined to be a beggar his whole life, all because people didn't understand the purpose of God in his life.

Jesus bent down and spit in the dirt, stirred it all up with his finger. Then scooped it up in his hand and smeared it all over the man's eyes. It's a good thing the man was blind. I'm not sure how a seeing man would have reacted to such an act, but that is what Jesus did. Then he told the man to go to the pool of Pool of Siloam, a gentle pool, not a rushing river but a quiet place, and wash his eyes.

Someone had to lead him to the pool. He was blind from birth and probably didn't even know where this pool was or how to get there, but he found someone to take him, and they went. When he got there, he washed his eyes and suddenly he could see. Some historians believe that he may have actually stepped down into the pool of Siloam and washed his whole body, as it was an enormous pool.

Interesting. Why wash in the pool of Siloam, and why dip in the Jordan? Both signify new beginnings, but a more profound answer lies in the treasure of who Jesus is.

Zachariah 4:6
Then he answered and spake unto me, saying, This is the word of Jehovah unto Zerubbabel, saying, Not by might, nor by power, but by my Spirit, saith Jehovah of hosts. ASV

It's not by our might or our reasoning. Nor can we, by our own efforts, power, education, or wisdom, bring about a man's deliverance. But it is by the Spirit of the Lord. It is not even something we can truly understand in our finite brains, as our mentality can not even fathom the darkness, say nothing of all the reasons why, but we can go forward. We can take our gaze from the past and stop asking why and focus on our future! Lord, what would you have me do today? What must I do to be healed? Where can I find peace today? What treasures have you hidden in this dark place for me to find?

And when you find that treasure, like the pearl of great price Jesus spoke of, you sell all to buy it. Whatever you have to do to get your treasure, you do it. Even if it means you dip in the muddy water seven times and take your spit

and mud encrusted eyes to the pool and wash. You let the
funny man of God pray for you, and find your treasure.
Then carry it out of your darkness. How long does it take?
I don't know. It depends on the volume of treasure the
Lord has hidden inside of your darkness.

Matthew 13:44-46
*The kingdom of heaven is like unto a treasure hidden in
the field; which a man found, and hid; and in his joy he
goeth and selleth all that he hath, and buyeth that field.
Again, the kingdom of heaven is like unto a man that is a
merchant seeking goodly pearls:
and having found one pearl of great price, he went and sold
all that he had, and bought it. ASV*

Chapter 11
Finding God

Sitting on the cement floor watching people as they cried out to God, I noticed one girl in particular. She was sobbing in the arms of my niece, Angelina. Later the next day, Angelina told me the girl's story. She had run away from her home on the island of Palawan and had gotten a job in Manila. The truth was, she hadn't just run away from home, but she was running from God as well. She got a job as a housemaid for an older woman. One night when she was sleeping, her boss's son came home high on drugs. He entered her second-floor bedroom and stabbed her twenty-eight times. She struggled with the man, and despite her injuries, she ran to the window and jumped. She survived the attack but spent weeks in the hospital and eventually returned home to Palawan. The night we saw her, she was crying, asking God to help her forgive that man. The next morning, she handed Angelina a note that said she had finally released all of her unforgiveness and pain to God and that now she was so much lighter and finally, after many months, she felt free.

Not only did she find freedom from all the pain she experienced from the attack, but she drew close to God. She was happy to be home, and was even happier that because of all the suffering and pain she had gone through, she had developed a relationship with God that she never dreamed was possible. She saw herself differently. It was the voice of God that had changed her that night. She had found a treasure in her darkness.

Often when we suffer, we feel alone. We don't feel loved, and we have feelings of rejection. These feelings not only cut us off from family and friends but also cause us to lose the feeling of God's presence. Often when we try to express our thoughts and explain what we are going through, we feel like no one understands. Shutting ourselves into our own mental prison, we yearn for God's presence and feel the despair of loneliness. It is in these moments that we experience dark places. Too often, our first inclination is to burrow even deeper into our pain, hoping to protect ourselves. When what we really should do is look for treasure.

So how do we dig for treasure? First, we have to learn how to talk to God. It is most important when looking for treasure, but many people have never developed this ability. Have you ever heard someone say, "I don't know how to pray?" Most people who say this have never truly entered into a talking relationship with God, and don't know that prayer is simply talking to God. They don't know how to pray, because they think it is harder than it is, so after a few attempts, they quit, believing they are doing it all wrong. Just talk to God. Tell him how you feel. Don't try to overthink it. Don't worry about the words you use.

We live in an insta-matic society and few people understand the importance of spending time in prayer. We have instant coffee, steaks, soup, frozen dinners and popcorn. Sermons in some churches are often delegated to fifteen or twenty-minute time segments, not escaping the time constraints most common in an instant society. Television shows that once took an hour to watch are reduced to the minutes left after all the commercials that promise instant results, instant hair growth, whiter teeth, or weight loss. We have lost the respect and value of time. It takes time to develop the skills necessary to become a master craftsman, to create works of art, or to accomplish something of value, and prayer is no different. Time is essential in searching for treasure. If you don't take the time to do it, if you don't take time to really look and pursue treasure, you will never find it.

I have watched people with metal detectors scouring beaches and the grounds of abandoned buildings. I noticed these people get up early and start searching before anybody else is around. Sometimes they search all day until dark. They spend time, lots of time. How much time do you invest in prayer, digging for your treasure? Have you turned off the TV just to talk with God? The noise of life demands our attention, but those who are serious about treasure hunting refuse to be sidelined. They are determined to find their treasure.

The prophet Isaiah understood that a person with seeing eyes, hearing ears, and a tender-understanding heart could turn to God and receive healing. Jesus even quoted Isaiah in Matthew 13:14-16. He emphasized their importance in receiving miracles, understanding God's Word, and the

Secrets of the Kingdom of Heaven. (Matthew 13:11). It was as if Jesus was saying, "if you master these, you are guaranteed to find treasure."

Matthew 13:11
And he answered and said unto them, Unto you it is given to know the mysteries of the kingdom of heaven, but to them it is not given. ASV

I remember my dad saying, "Look at me when I talk to you." He expected my full attention when he was speaking. I have said the same thing in the last few years, only more so in this digital world. It seems everyone is on their phone or device. Paying attention is a lost art. School teachers, pastors, and public speakers have a hard time keeping their audience's attention because they can't compete with the speed devices used to captivate their watchers. We have to re-learn the ability to see.

Some people seem to have a real knack for finding things. I happen to be one of them, I can find things no one else can. My dad called me one day after he and my mom had searched throughout the house looking for his cell phone. They both declared they had searched and searched, and just couldn't find it. So I drove over to their house and asked my dad where he thought he saw it last. When he told me he thought it was in his bedroom, I walked up the stairs, opened the door and there was his phone. It was laying in a rumpled blanket that had been tossed on the floor during their search.

Another time I was shopping with my husband Fred. He needed new dress shoes and had found a pair that he liked, but when he took them out of the box, they were two different sizes. He had looked and looked throughout the racks of shoes and couldn't find the mate to the shoe he wanted, and even asked a store clerk to help him. When he came to me with his sad story, I said, "Give me the shoe box. I'll find your missing shoe." I walked to the shoe department and immediately my eyes fell on a box that held another pair of mix-mated shoes. It took me maybe thirty seconds to find the missing shoe. You might find this unbelievable, but it is true. I find things. I know how to "see." How did I get this gift? I asked God for it. Every time I ask, I find. I find missing money, eyeglasses, books, you name it, I've found it.

Treasure hunters need eyes to see what is lost. They need to take the time to search and they need to see what they are looking for. Open your spiritual eyes and see what you can't find. See with God's eyes. What treasure are you looking for? Close your eyes and see the son or daughter who is lost. See the vision you have forgotten. Fix your eyes on your treasure and see through the rubble of your life. See through the drug addiction of your child's life. See through the alcoholism, see through the hate, the bitterness, and the fear. When I was a child, I used to watch Superman. Not the sophisticated version we see today in the movies, just Clark Kent, who worked at the Daily Planet newspaper. There were several supernatural things he could do. He could fly and was stronger than anyone else. Another thing he could do was to see as he had X-ray vision. He would fix his eyes in such a way that he could see through walls. We need spiritual X-ray vision. Do something with me right now. Close your eyes and imagine the treasures if you are seeking. Imagine seeing your husband saved, your wife healed, your children delivered. Imagine your finances in order, your job situation changed.

Then as you see them - pray, "Lord, I see the treasure in my husband, wife, boss, child. I see what you want for their life. I see the treasure. Teach me how to dig it out. Teach me, Lord. I want my treasure. I'll do whatever it takes."

If you meant it, watch out. God will move heaven and earth to work with you. See the heavenly bulldozers, big earth movers coming towards your situation and pushing the sickness, poverty, drug addictions away.

Isaiah 6:10 tells us that people who have closed eyes and ears, and who have a hard heart, can not understand God or His ways. Matthew repeats Isaiah, but also says that if we see with our eyes and hear with our ears, and understand with our hearts, we can be healed. In other words, seeing eyes, hearing ears and tender hearts are ready for healing, deliverance, provision, and restoration.

Isaiah 6:10
Make the heart of this people fat, and make their ears heavy, and shut their eyes; lest they see with their eyes, and hear with their ears, and understand with their heart, and turn again, and be healed. ASV

Matthew 13:14-16
And unto them is fulfilled the prophecy of Isaiah, which saith, By hearing ye shall hear, and shall in no wise understand; And seeing ye shall see, and shall in no wise perceive:

For this people's heart is waxed gross, And their ears are dull of hearing, And their eyes they have closed; Lest haply they should perceive with their eyes, And hear with their ears, And understand with their heart, And should turn again, And I should heal them.
But blessed are your eyes, for they see; and your ears, for they hear. ASV

We need hearing ears because prayer is not just talking but also listening. This world is full of noise. Some we hear and some we don't hear. There are all kinds of sounds, sounds we can hear and sounds we can't. All kinds of animals such as whales, pigeons, and hippos, and elephants use low-frequency sounds to interact. These sounds are so low a human can not hear them, but these animals can hear them up to two and a half miles away. Why? Because they have an internal ear that is tuned to that frequency. Our phones, televisions, radios, and other equipment are tuned to sounds we can not hear with our ears, and yet the sound is real, and we can hear that sound because we have devises tuned in.

It is the same in the spiritual dimension. We need to be tuned in to the Holy Spirit, and the only way to do that is time. I knew my dad's voice because I spent time with him. My sister knows my voice because we spend time together. Anytime you spend time with someone, you develop an ear to hear. The Bible talks about having an ear to hear what the Spirit is saying, and it is essential to have a hearing ear to find treasure in the dark places. Sometimes it is so dark you can't see your hand before your face, but you can hear.

Finally, we need hearts that understand. We need a tender heart that is open to what God is saying, a heart that will change and turn around. A heart that says, "I'll do anything God wants me to in order to find my treasure. I'll pay any price to see a change in my life. I'll open up my heart and love the unlovely, forgive the unforgivable, and embrace the unwanted. God will work his miracles in my life when I dig for treasure with everything that is in me. I may experience trouble, but the trouble will not destroy me. Persecution may come, but I am not dismayed. I'm not abandoned or destroyed. I am a TREASURE hunter!"

2 Corinthians 4:7-9
And we have this treasure in earthen vessels, that the excellency of the power may be of God, and not of us; on every side being in tribulation, but not straitened; perplexed, but not in despair; persecuted, but not forsaken; cast down, but not destroyed; YLT

I hope this book has encouraged you to think about your dark times differently. There are many hard places in life, and I could not address them all. But I hope that you have discovered that treasures exist in all the dark places you may travel through. These abundant riches have been set aside just for you. Don't give up. Never leave your dark place without the treasured reward that is yours.

Debby

Books by Debby:

Suddenly
Keepers of Salt
Keepers of Salt Study Guide
The Only Way Out Is In
Peace
Because God Said So
Dog of Blue
Any Old Bush
The Storm Walker
An Agent of God
Creatures of The Forest
Ruth
Crackers
Rosie
Emma and Friends
Treasures In Dark Places

If you would like to have Debby speak to your church,
Bible Study, or other gathering contact her at
debby@davismission.com

Made in the USA
Middletown, DE
24 October 2023

41366992R00068